Designing Usable Apps

An agile approach to User Experience design

Kevin Matz

WinchelseaPress

Designing Usable Apps: An agile approach to User Experience design

Published by
Winchelsea Press
an imprint of Winchelsea Systems Ltd.
Calgary, Alberta, Canada

ISBN: 978-0-9869109-0-6

Version: Print-1.0 (2013.09.22)
10 9 8 7 6 5 4 3 2 1

Winchelsea Press and Winchelsea Systems are trademarks of Winchelsea Systems Ltd.
Winchelsea Press is not associated with any other product or vendor mentioned in this
book, and any trademarks are the property of their respective owners.

Visit us at:

www.designingusableapps.com
www.winchelseapress.com
www.winchelseasystems.com

Contact the author at: **kevin@winchelseasystems.com**

With thanks to Ron, Maia, and Laura,
for their support and encouragement

Contents

8

User skill levels and skill acquisition

9

The fundamentals of human-computer interaction

10

Design principles for usability   111

11

Creating a positive user experience   123

12

Designing your application's interaction concept   127

13

Designing the visual appearance   143

14

15

16

Designing auxiliary and cross-cutting aspects   209

17

Usability testing and evaluation   227

1

Introduction

Only a few decades ago, computers were giant machines that were so expensive that they could only be acquired by large corporations and universities. Computer time was considered more valuable than the time of the human operators, economically speaking, and so this meant that users had to structure their work to conform to the needs of the computer.

In fact, during the early ages of mainframe computing, the interaction between users and computers was minimized to the point where most users never even got to touch the machine. You'd have to write out a program listing, encode it onto punched cards, and then hand your cards to an operator who would schedule an opportunity to feed your batch of cards into the machine. The next day, you'd stand in line to pick up your printout.

Needless to say, technological advancements have radically changed the way we interact with computing devices today. The inexpensiveness of computing power and the opportunities created by networking devices together have introduced computing and software into almost every facet of everyday life, changing the way we work, play, communicate, and socialize.

As technology and software have become pervasive, our expectations for how it should work have changed accordingly. Users must no longer be highly-trained specialists. We expect our gadgets and apps to continually surprise us with more and more magic, and we expect do less and less manual work and thinking. We expect to be able to pick up a device or download an app and start using it right away without reading a manual. And we expect apps and websites to be visually appealing and fun to use.

In other words, we increasingly expect machines to conform to our natural human ways of thinking and working, rather than the other way around.

Whether you're designing a desktop app, a mobile app, a tablet app, a website, a web application, or a large business enterprise system, creating a great experience for your users and customers is an important investment. Neglecting usability concerns is no longer a realistic option if you want your product to be commercially successful.

For consumer-oriented apps, games, and websites, the marketplace is becoming increasingly crowded. To attract and retain users and remain competitive, your product must provide a rich and compelling user experience and must be easy to learn and use.

For enterprise applications — the software that runs an organization's operations — attention to usability can increase employees' productivity, decrease error rates, reduce training costs, boost morale, reduce staff turnover, and minimize helpdesk and tech support costs.

Designing usable software products is more of an art than a science. Fortunately, it is an art that can be learned, and this book will help you learn how to do it.

Who is this book for?

If you're involved in any way in the design and creation of software products or websites, and you want to learn how to make your product more enjoyable and efficient to use, then this book is for you.

You may have a job title such as product manager, project manager, developer, user interface designer, user experience designer, interaction designer, graphic designer, web designer, usability specialist, business analyst, requirements engineer, or QA specialist. Or you might even be a one-person startup exploring a market opportunity.

In many large organizations, the people who end up designing software applications are subject matter experts who know the business domain and business processes well, but don't have a technical or software development background and may not be familiar with basic ideas and terminology involved in designing software applications and user interfaces. If you fall into this category, this book will serve as a useful introduction to software design and the principles of usability.

What is this book about?

In this book, you'll learn about what makes software products easy and fun to learn and use, and what things can cause users to become frustrated.

You'll learn about understanding your users and customers, and discovering what they want and need from your product.

You'll learn how to investigate, plan, and design all of the key aspects of the user-facing part of a software product, including information architecture, data modelling, visual design, and interaction design. You'll learn about exploring design alternatives, and you'll learn recommended techniques for specifying and communicating your designs.

You'll also learn techniques for evaluating and testing that your designs and your product are usable.

And you'll learn how to integrate usability activities into a software project.

What is this book not about?

This is a book about designing software, but it doesn't cover the technical aspects — the architectural design and programming — that are needed to make a design a reality.

And while this book is about designing software that meets market needs, it makes no attempt to be a comprehensive guide to software marketing.

Why this book?

There are plenty of other books on usability and software design on the market. Why read this one?

- This is the only book that I'm aware of that intentionally integrates data and domain modeling, information architecture, visual design, and interaction design together into a coherent approach to software product design.

- It's practical and action-oriented. We'll start by exploring some fundamental ideas and concepts, and then we'll discover concrete techniques that you can use for planning and executing a software design project. It guides you through all of the aspects you need to consider and all of the techniques you'll need to use when planning and designing a new software product.

- It's compact and to-the-point. The text has been aggressively edited and trimmed to be focused and relevant. The page count has intentionally been kept relatively low so that you'll be encouraged to read the whole book.

One of the main ideas of this book is that usability problems often emerge because designers don't sufficiently think through all of the issues that need to be considered when creating a product that meets the needs of users and customers. This book can thus serve as a checklist of all of the various things you need to think about and decide on when creating and designing a new software product.

Let's get started!

2

Defining usability and user experience (UX)

If our goal is to create usable software, let's start by thinking about what we mean by terms like *usability* and *user experience (UX)*.

A software product that is **usable**:

- can be learned easily,

- can be operated efficiently, and

- provides a generally pleasant experience when used.

Judging the usability of a product or a design is often difficult because each of these three criteria is subjective, with each criteria depending to a great degree on the individual user operating the product. Different users could often have very different experiences with a product, as each user will have a unique background with a set of skills, knowledge, and past experiences. Each user's expectations, opinions, and preferences affect how the product will be perceived. Some users are more curious, patient, and persistent than others when faced with a problem or a new situation. And users' experiences can further be affected by moods, stress, fatigue, distractions, and the opinions of people around them.

Although the three primary usability criteria are subjective, it is nevertheless still worthwhile to delve into factors for each criteria.

Learnability

A product tends to be *easy to learn* if:

- the operations and functions that the product provides are clearly evident, with appropriate controls and labels clearly visible;

- possible navigation destinations and the user's current location are clearly presented;

- there is a minimum of memorization and recall required, and any commands or action sequences are easily memorable;

- the product encourages exploration and experimentation;

- it is easy to undo mistakes and retry operations;

- help and assistance are easily accessible when needed, and the help information is clear, correct, and relevant;

- terminology, visual layout, and behavior are consistent, allowing the user to detect patterns and form an accurate mental model of how the product works;

- there are few or no surprises or "exceptions to the rule" to discover and memorize;

- wherever possible, the user is guided step-by-step through complex tasks;

- when the user performs an action, the product provides clear feedback;

- the status of the system is clearly presented;

- the product conforms to generally-accepted standards (for example, a Windows application adheres to the guidelines and standards of the operating system); and

- everything is as simple as possible and all parts of the system make sense together as a coherent whole.

Efficiency

A product can be used *efficiently* if:

- it is easy for an experienced user to remember how to perform actions and complete tasks without having to look up instructions;

- the user can complete routine tasks without much conscious thinking and deliberation;

- the product enables and encourages users to enter a "flow" state of high focus, productivity, and creativity;

- the product allows a skilled user to achieve a low error rate, and any mistakes can be easily detected and corrected;

- the product's performance and stability are sufficient to prevent delays and interruptions that hinder the flow of work; and

- there are no unexpected surprises and inconsistencies.

Pleasantness of the experience

Using a product can be a *pleasant experience* when:

- the product is aesthetically pleasing to look at;

- for a productivity application or business system, it enables productive work to be done efficiently;

- for a game, it provides enjoyment, challenge or distraction, and entertainment value;

- the user feels rewarded as tasks and actions are completed;

- the product is stable, reliable, and trustworthy;

- the product's performance (e.g., response time) is sufficient to avoid delays and frustration;

- the product is ergonomically comfortable; and

- the product is free of unnecessary annoyances and frustrations.

We should add that for many entertainment and game products, novelty or uniqueness can contribute to a satisfying experience as well.

What is user experience (UX)?

The entire experience — including positive or negative emotional reactions and feelings of satisfaction or dissatisfaction — that a user or customer gets from using a software product or computing device is so important that we have a special name for it: **user experience**, or "**UX**".

User experience is shaped by more than just the look and feel of a product's user interface. The scope of the product's features and functionality is important as well: What problems can the product solve? What work can it help the user achieve, or what entertainment value does it provide?

For physical products like a mobile phone, the industrial design and build quality of the device, and even the product packaging, contribute to the overall experience. For a software application, the acquisition process (e.g., downloading and installing an app) is part of the experience as well. The user experience is also shaped by the branding and visual design, the marketing and advertising materials, the website, and any documentation or collateral materials.

If the user must call a technical support hotline for assistance or to register and activate the product, then this interaction with your organization's staff also forms part of your product's user experience.

If the product enables communication or social interaction with other people, or if the user feels that the product enhances their status or prestige, then these things can be considered part of the overall user experience as well.

And does the user or customer feel that the product provides good value for the money spent on it? Yes, even that contributes to the user's overall impressions and experience with your product.

So while this book concentrates on the design of software user interfaces, there's often much more to creating a great user experience than just making the user interface attractive and usable. If you're planning to design and launch a new product, you need to think about all of the things that the user will see and interact with, and you need to design all of these things to provide the best experience possible, within your budget and timeline.

User experience as a factor in the acceptability of a product

The usability of a product and the likability of its user experience play a part in the user's or customer's determination of whether the product is *acceptable*. Shackel (1991) argues that users find a product to be acceptable when its utility — the functions it performs — and its usability and likability are judged to be sufficient in relation to the costs involved in acquiring, learning, and using the product.

If a product is not deemed to be acceptable, users and customers will seek alternatives in the marketplace. Thus, to make your product competitive and increase the chances of commercial success, careful attention to user experience design is important.

3

What is involved in designing a software product and its user interface?

Designing a software product and its user interface is, you'd might think, just a matter of deciding what controls will be on the screen, arranging the controls, and figuring out what should happen when the user interacts with the controls. While that's not incorrect, there's also more to it than that. To design a product's user interface effectively, you typically have to think through and decide on all of the following:

- What is the scope of the product's functionality? In other words, what tasks and activities can a user perform with the application?

- How will the interaction proceed for each task? What steps and actions shall the user perform, and what steps and actions shall the product perform?

- What is the overall visual style or appearance of the application? What will the basic page templates or screen layouts look like, and what fonts, colors, iconography, and branding will be used?

- What "places" are there in the application? By *places*, we mean discrete locations like pages in a web application, screens and dialogs and panels in a desktop or mobile application, or even levels in a game.

- How does the user navigate between the places?

- What content and layout will be present in each place? What controls and objects are available, and how are they arranged?

- By what means can the controls be manipulated or activated (e.g., clicking or dragging with the mouse, or touch gestures on a touch display), and what behavior occurs during each such event?

- What events does the application have to deal with that aren't triggered by the user? For example, do timer-driven events occur, or does the application react to information arriving from another system?

- What data or content does the application store, manage, and present? How is it represented on the screen?

- What names or labels will you use to refer to all the things (places, data elements, objects, controls, concepts, and so on) in your application?

- When errors occur, how will the user be informed of the situation, and what opportunities will the user have to correct or recover from the errors?

- Are there different roles or classifications of users? What actions are permitted or not permitted for each role?

- How will users get assistance when they face a problem or are unsure of how to accomplish a task? Will you make available help content, reference documentation, tutorials, videos, technical support hotlines, web-based discussion forums, or searchable knowledge bases?

- How will you structure the application to guide new users through tasks and help them figure out how the application works?

In order to make decisions and design something for each of these points, you'll have to engage in requirements gathering and analysis: You'll need to understand who will be using your product, what their characteristics are, and what they want and need from your product. Most software applications solve some problem or assist in doing a specific type of work, and so you'll need to understand the work, the tasks, and the problem domain. And to some degree, you'll need to understand the technology requirements, because the choice of technologies for building the product will need to meet those requirements, and the choice of technologies can in some cases have an enormous impact on the design and the effectiveness of the user interface.

And since you're probably working in a team, you'll have to communicate your designs and intentions to the team members who will build and test the product. This communication can take the form of prototypes and mockups, formal design documents and specifications, face-to-face communication in front of a whiteboard, or some combination of these.

As well, you will need to be sure that what you design is feasible within the constraints of your project: It has to be implementable using your technical framework, it must be implementable with the skills of the team members available, and it must be implementable within the time and budget constraints of your project. Additionally, the product's performance must be acceptable. And if the product is being marketed (as opposed to being a one-off custom project for a client), will the product sell enough copies to be profitable?

We should note that the things we've discussed may not necessarily all be performed or decided upon by one single designer. In mid- to large-sized project teams, multiple people in different roles will take responsibility for different analysis and design tasks. Tasks might be divided amongst people with job titles such as product managers, requirements analysts, business analysts, information architects, user interface or UX designers, usability specialists, developers, and so on. If your product is being developed for a particular niche or industry, such as banking or insurance or air traffic control, specialists with knowledge and experience in that domain — Subject Matter Experts, or SMEs — will also play a key role in defining and designing the product.

4

Structuring software projects for usability

Software products are created in software projects, and whether you have a large project team, or you're a one-person startup, the way you structure your project can have an enormous impact on your ability to deliver a usable product. Let's take a look at how to structure and manage software projects so that usability-related activities are properly integrated.

Project management approaches

The traditional textbook approach to designing and building software products has been the *waterfall model*, in which the first major phase of the project is dedicated to gathering requirements and recording them in specifications documents. These are then handed off to designers and architects, who create design specifications. These are then handed off to developers, who build the product. The product is then handed off to testers, who verify that the product matches the specifications.

At a distance, this is a very logical, rational, sequential decomposition, but it is also a vast oversimplification. In most large, real-life projects, it's never possible for analysts and designers and programmers to get everything correct and complete on the first try, and so most waterfall projects usually tend to break down into a chaotic scene of documents and artifacts being passed back and forth between groups for correction. And since software projects span months or years, it's very possible that the requirements will change during the course of the project, meaning that by the time the product is finally built and released, it may no longer actually meet the needs of the users and stakeholders.

An more effective way of bringing some order to this process is to recognize that complex analysis, design, and development work is never done completely or correctly on the first attempt; it takes many iterations of reviewing, revising, and testing to get it right. And so an *iterative approach* breaks the project into many short, structured cycles of work. At the beginning of each cycle, or iteration, the focus of the effort can be redefined to match the current priorities and to take into account the current state of the project. And with each iteration, the work products get better and more complete.

When using the iterative approach, the usual strategy is to always have an actual working version of the software ready at the end of each iteration (although in the earliest iterations, this might take the form of plans or prototypes). An advantage to this approach is that you get a very basic version of the product available for testing very early on in the project, and this early demonstration version can be used to discuss and further refine requirements with the project stakeholders.

An approach that combines the idea of iteration with the active involvement of users in the project is *User-Centered Design*.

What is User-Centered Design?

User-Centered Design (UCD) is an approach to software design that encourages the active involvement of real users during all stages of the project. Gould and Lewis's 1985 paper *Designing for usability: Key principles and what designers think* identifies the three components of the UCD philosophy:

1. *An early focus on understanding users and tasks*

    The designers and developers should have direct contact with actual or prospective users, so that the users and their tasks can be understood. This is especially important at the beginning of the project, but improving your understanding of the users and their requirements should also be an ongoing effort throughout the project.

2. *Early and continual user testing with empirical measurement*

    Throughout the project, users should be involved in validating the user requirements and evaluating product designs.

    Evaluations can be done by observing users as they interact with the product or a prototype of the product. You can obtain qualitative data by recording users' experiences and reactions and asking for feedback. Deeper insights can be obtained from quantitative data: you can define metrics for usability factors like learnability, efficiency, and error rates, and then measure and compare users' performance across different versions of prototypes.

Continual user testing helps ensure that the product is on track, and reveals usability problems and defects in your designs and prototypes.

3. *Iterative design*

   The product should undergo a repeating cycle of analysis, design, modification, and testing. Each cycle offers the opportunity to fix usability problems that have been identified, and to incorporate changes resulting from gaining an improved understanding of the users' requirements.

A later 1991 paper by Gould, Boies, and Lewis added the following fourth aspect:

4. *Integrated design*

   The various aspects of the product that contribute to usability — i.e., the conceptual design, user interface design, documentation, training, help system, etc. — are all tightly interrelated. For example, a change in the conceptual model will require changes in the user interface, which will then require updates to the help system.

   They should therefore evolve together in parallel and be under the same management. Otherwise, if some aspects are placed under the management of another organizational department (e.g., a Training and Documentation department), or in a separate sequential project phase, coordination problems will tend to result.

Structuring project iterations for User-Centered Design

There are many ways to structure the general flow of work within an iterative cycle. For the purposes of user interface design, a general approach for an iteration of the design cycle usually ends up looking something like Figure 4-1.

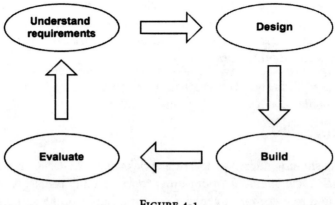

FIGURE 4-1

Users and other stakeholders will be involved in the "Understand requirements" activity, where you work to discover what the system must do to meet users' needs. Users can provide information and opinions, answer questions, and help validate or disprove any assumptions that you make. (In Chapter 6, we'll explore the process of gathering and analyzing product and user requirements.)

During the "Design" and "Build" activities, users can be consulted to get feedback and opinions on the appearance and workings of the proposed product or enhancements. If users can help catch design flaws and identify false assumptions at this stage, it can save time, as it is easier to change a design than to rework software that has already been built. (The process of design is the focus of most of the later chapters in this book.)

Once some set of features has been constructed, the "Evaluate" activity involves inspecting the software. In the simplest case, software testing can be conducted to ensure the software matches the design and the requirements. Ideally, users should help validate that the software meets their needs (or is on track to provide the functionality required). Users should also be involved in usability testing activities. Additionally, you may also wish to measure metrics to track progression and identify trends over multiple iterations. (Metrics will be discussed in Chapter 6, and techniques for conducting usability evaluations and testing will be covered in Chapter 17.)

The findings from evaluation activities will identify problems, generate further ideas for developing the product, and help the team decide upon the highest priority tasks to tackle in the next iteration. Evaluation activities tend to lead to a better understanding of the requirements, or can identify potential new or changed requirements that need to be analyzed and understood, and so the cycle repeats anew.

The above diagram is unsatisfying, though: it suggests that the activities are separate and take place sequentially, and this is not always the case. There is often constant, fluid switching between the different activities, and team members will often be working on different activities simultaneously in parallel.

In addition, the nature of different products can enable various different design approaches:

- For products with formal processes and very specific externally-imposed requirements, such as a tax calculator, requirements analysis and specification usually have to be figured out fairly thoroughly before detailed design can proceed.

- On the other end of the spectrum, products such as games have few critical functional requirements — just about anything goes, design-wise, as long as the game is fun to play — and so traditional requirements analysis virtually disappears.

- Most products fit somewhere in the middle, and requirements analysis and design proceed together in a tightly meshed, overlapping fashion. Sometimes requirements aren't formally recorded at all, and instead the design is simply continually adjusted to match the new learnings about how the product should work. So in these cases, the "Understand requirements" and "Design" activities would merge together.

And for products that lend themselves to rapid prototyping, it is possible that no formal design documentation is ever recorded. The prototype is the entire representation of the design, and so in that case, the "Design" and "Build" activities would merge together.

We should also note that the diagram in Figure 4-1 has many similarities to the Build-Measure-Learn process cycle promoted by the Lean Startup methodology (Ries, 2011), which is extremely useful for discovering and validating a profitable product-market opportunity.

Overcoming objections to User-Centered Design

Although the basic ideas underlying the User-Centered Design approach make a lot of sense, in many traditional corporate environments, there can be extraordinary management resistance to involving users in the product development process and employing a strategy of iterative refinement. Let's examine some common objections to UCD and how you might address them.

- *"We don't need to talk to users. The team already has experts with all the knowledge needed to design the product."*

You'd be surprised at what you can learn from observing users doing their work, asking what problems they have with their current system or approach, and getting their ideas on what could be done better. It's virtually guaranteed to challenge some of your long-held assumptions.

For enterprise applications, it is often assumed that it is sufficient to interview a handful of experts, and perhaps the managers who oversee the users. But it's important to talk to the actual users who will actually work with the product or system. Workers frequently deal with problems and special cases that require workarounds, and managers may overlook these issues, downplay them, or may not even be aware of them.

- *"We have a very tight schedule. We can't afford to waste time talking to users and involving them in evaluations and testing."*

Getting the requirements right is important so that you build the right product. This will help ensure customer satisfaction, improve the chances of market success, and will prevent the team from wasting valuable time on unnecessary features and rework.

Likewise, testing the product as it is developed to ensure that it really meets the users' needs will avoid costly disputes with the customer (for bespoke enterprise systems) or failure in the marketplace (for consumer products) after the product is delivered.

- *"We don't want to lose face in front of our customers if our team members ask stupid questions that we should already know the answers to."*

Users and customers are usually more impressed that the team cares enough to take the time to understand their needs. By assigning experienced senior staff to be involved with the users, you may be able to avoid any potentially embarrassing situations.

- *"If we involve our users and stakeholders, they will all have different ideas and opinions that will divert our project's focus off track."*

Ensure that all proposed requirements undergo a proper review process to ensure that everyone's wished-for features don't gradually sneak into the product scope (this is known as **scope creep** or **requirements leakage**) without analysis and confirmation by an authority. A checklist-based review process such as the **Quality Gateway** described in the textbook *Mastering the Requirements Process* (Robertson and Robertson, 2012) is recommended for managing product scope and for controlling the quality of proposed requirements.

- *"This approach violates our standard project management methodology."*

If you're forced to use a company-wide standard project methodology, ask whether the status-quo approach has always delivered flawless results, or whether there's potential room for improvement. Providing a concrete example or case study of how user testing or iterative refinement would have avoided a problem can be a powerful strategy for making the case for the value of an alternative approach.

Many middle managers are extremely risk-averse, and so by permitting any approach that they consider new, unfamiliar, or unconventional, they would be exposing themselves to blame if anything goes wrong (whereas "going by the book" reduces the risk of being blamed for a project failure). If you find yourself dealing with this situation, you can try to fit the new approach into your company's standard approach, for example, by introducing usability testing in some limited way.

In one project I was involved in, the company's management was adamantly opposed to agile and iterative methodologies. However, my project plan was approved when, instead of referring to "iterations", I described the project strategy in terms of a series of short project phases, where the project plan would be systematically reviewed and readjusted at the beginning of each phase based on the current state of the project at that stage. This is, of course, largely the same thing as an agile and iterative approach, but described in more comfortable, traditional terms.

- *"We don't have staff experienced in these user-centered techniques."*

Designers and developers can learn techniques from books or training courses, or you might consider hiring a usability consultant.

- *"Marketing is responsible for talking to the customers."*

Many organizations suffer from unproductive conflicts between competing managers and departments over their areas of responsibility. Try to establish partnerships and good working relationships with other teams, and build consensus around the need to establish the best process for ensuring a quality product, as all departments will benefit if the product is successful.

- *"By talking to users, we risk leaking secrets."*

Confidentiality is an important concern during product development, as there is fear of competitors learning about product strategy or technical details of the product's unique differentiating features (the "secret sauce"). Consider non-disclosure agreements. Or, if possible, instead of working with users at your customers' sites or recruiting users "off the street", you may (depending on your type of product) be able to compromise by finding representative users within your own organization.

- *"I don't want someone on our team to make promises to customers that we can't keep."*

Ensure that users and customers understand that their suggestions and feedback are important, and that the project will try to accommodate as many reasonable ideas as possible, but that management will decide on the project scope, and no guarantees can be made for any particular feature requests. Explain that the project has deadline and budget constraints and must satisfy multiple stakeholders, and that compromises must be reached. You may also again want to let your most senior staff interact with the users.

- *"We can't afford to test with users. They might find a fatal flaw that will impact our deadlines!"*

Much better to find any serious flaws early, when they can be corrected, than to discover them after delivering the product!

Winning support for usability activities in enterprise application projects

One class of software that is particularly notorious for usability problems is enterprise software. Companies marketing products to consumers understand that investing resources in creating a good user experience can pay for itself through increased sales and revenues. But the economics are different for custom enterprise applications built by an organization for its own internal use. Typically, no direct revenue stream results from the application, and so there is immense pressure to minimize costs. Since enterprise applications are only used by an organization's internal staff and not the general public, the users will be asked to tolerate imperfect software in order to keep the costs as low as possible. The usability situation becomes worse when multiple aging, complex, unreliable systems are then cobbled together in systems integration projects.

If you are in the position of trying to win management support for investing in usability activities for a custom enterprise application project, you must usually make an argument on economic grounds. Because the potential for increasing revenues can be ruled out (making a unique one-off system better won't increase revenues because no more copies will be sold), you'll have to make the case on the basis of cost savings, arguing that more usable software will:

- increase productivity, reduce errors and mistakes, and minimize users' wasted time;

- reduce support and helpdesk inquiries;

- reduce the number of change requests in the future and save on maintenance and redevelopment efforts; and,

- improve staff morale and possibly reduce staff turnover.

While the potential cost savings can be real, they are also impossible to precisely quantify. The cost savings are also spread out over the long term. Thus, unfortunately, putting together a compelling case can be difficult.

How does poor design arise in products?

You can probably think of many products that you've purchased or used that have not met your expectations. Why do some products have such a disappointing user experience? It's a question worth exploring, since we'd like to avoid these mistakes when designing and building a new product.

For a product that has a disappointing user experience, there was likely a combination of some of the following problems at the organization that produced it:

- Not enough attention was paid to explicitly designing the user experience during product development; the design just haphazardly emerged.

- Research to understand the wants and needs of users was not performed, or user research was done but the user requirements were disregarded in the product design and development.

- Time and budget constraints didn't allow enough time and resources for proper design, implementation, and testing.

- The choice of technology (such as the framework for constructing the user interface) did not meet the actual requirements, with the resulting limitations forcing compromises in the design and realization of the product.

- Technical architects and software developers who perhaps preferred to focus on the internal, technical aspects of the product were left to design the user interface, and a technology-driven design approach emerged instead of a user-centric design approach.

- Organizational politics led to unfortunate compromises.

- Usability testing was not performed, or it was performed too late in the project, and then the conclusions from the usability tests were not acted upon.

- Multiple designers worked on separate parts of the product and inconsistencies resulted because of a lack of coordination and collaboration.

- Incompetent people were involved in the management and implementation of the project.

If you are planning a project to develop a new product, you should be aware of these problems, and consciously develop strategies to avoid them.

5

Recording and communicating software designs

Designing software involves making decisions, solving problems, and creating conceptual structures. A large part of the process of design revolves around the need to record and communicate your decisions, findings, and designs in a way that is understandable to and consumable by stakeholders and team members, who will use the information as the basis for implementing, testing, and evaluating the product.

If you are a one-person team, and your product is not particularly large or complex, you may be able to envision the product in your head, and jump straight into implementing it without producing any sketches, diagrams, or documentation beforehand. This is "hacking", in the traditional, non-malicious sense of the word, and this can be very satisfying and productive, but there are limits to what one person can achieve alone.

Virtually all commercial software today is designed and built in teams of people, with team members having different roles and specializations. Collaboration and communication is necessary to keep the project on track to produce a coherent and successful product.

Communication and decisions can be permanently recorded in written records, documents, and diagrams, which we call **project artifacts**.

Two fundamental classes of artifacts for representing software designs are *documentation* and *prototypes*.

- **Documentation** artifacts can take many forms: text, diagrams, illustrations, models, matrices and spreadsheets, or information organized in a database. Documentation artifacts can describe either the current state of the world, or how the future product is intended to work. Documentation can describe things at various levels of abstraction and specificity.

- In contrast to documents, which describe something, a **prototype** expresses a design directly by serving as a working model of one or more aspects of the product. Prototypes help demonstrate what the product will look like and how it will behave, though prototypes are usually limited in one or more important aspects. But unlike documents, prototypes cannot explicitly express design intentions and rationale. In other words, prototypes cannot explain *why* something should look or behave the way that it does.

  Prototypes can exist at varying levels of detail and interactivity. **High-fidelity prototypes** are realistic-looking mockups, created as software or webpages that a user can interact with, although not all features will be supported, and results and behavioral flows may be simulated. **Low-fidelity prototypes** do not attempt to present a completely accurate visual representation, and can be as simple as rough sketches on paper.

Many projects rely solely on documentation artifacts. Some projects will benefit from a combination of documentation and prototypes, and for products of significant complexity, neither alone is sufficient. Prototypes are better for expressing things like visual design that are difficult to describe in words, and are useful for exploring and evaluating different design ideas.

But prototypes should not be used as the sole means of specification, because a prototype can contain inaccuracies that are not desired in the final product. A prototype may not contain a full implementation of complex logic or algorithms (or if it does, discovering and reverse-engineering the algorithms would be challenging). And if a prototype does implement rare or special cases, they may not be easily discoverable upon casual inspection.

Recording designs in documentation and prototype artifacts achieves the following:

- The artifacts serve as a means of communicating the design to your team members (and to other key stakeholders, such as your client, if you're working on a custom development project). Unlike informal face-to-face communication, artifacts are tangible and persistent. The design expressed by a document or prototype can be reviewed by team members, the clients, or users, to help ensure correctness and completeness before the costly and time-consuming process of construction begins. And the document or prototype communicates to developers and testers how the product should be built.

- The act of writing a document, drawing a diagram, or creating a prototype serves as a means of forcing you to arrange your thoughts into order. Many people think they have a complete concept in their head, but when they start describing it on paper, they realize that they have overlooked many important issues. By putting a design into permanent written form, you help trigger creativity, and it makes it easier to find holes in your logic. The act of recording your design helps you to generate a design that is concrete, complete, and conceptually coherent.

- By recording and explaining rationale for why certain decisions were made, you help create **traceability**, which can aid team members in understanding, implementing, and maintaining the design. By explaining the justifications behind the design decisions, you help prevent the time-wasting repetition of the investigation and decision-making process in the future.

Agile and lean documentation

Most people in software teams tend to dislike creating documentation, and so documentation in many projects is in a suboptimal state. Excessive time and energy is spent on documents that never get read. Documents often don't meet the information needs of the people relying on them; for instance, in some organizations, developers are often given specifications that are incomplete, inconsistent, or incoherent. The contents of documents often become out of date in the face of constant change, and no longer match what they are trying to describe. And, frankly, many people in the software industry are not particularly great at writing and communicating.

Although there is no easy answer to all of these problems, the best hope is the **agile documentation** approach, which applies concepts from agile software development and the "lean" movement to the tasks of producing and maintaining software project documentation in a practical, minimal, and efficient way.

In the *Agile Manifesto*, a statement of key values of the Agile movement, it is said that "working software" is valued over "comprehensive documentation". This is not to say that documentation is not valuable, but that at the end of a project, it is more important to have working software than it is to have perfect documentation. Agile documentation is thus a pragmatic, minimalist approach that states that documentation must directly serve the purpose of creating working software rather than being an end in itself.

Some of the key ideas of agile documentation are:

- Use simple, lightweight tools such as wikis that encourage informal collaboration with low overhead. The easier it is to create and update information, the more people will do so.

- When creating documentation, ensure that you have a clear, specific purpose. Think of the audience for each piece of documentation, and write with the reader's needs in mind.

- Creating documentation incurs a cost of time, effort, and wages. If the perceived benefit of the documentation does not outweigh the cost, reconsider whether the document is necessary. When considering the cost, keep in mind that many documents must be maintained and kept up-to-date over the long term.

- Avoid duplication, and don't document those obvious things that everyone already knows; concentrate more on documenting those things that are unusual or novel.

- Visuals such as diagrams, models, illustrations, and screen mockups can be more valuable than verbose textual descriptions, and working prototypes can be even more valuable.

- Consider the motto "just good enough, and just enough". Documentation doesn't have to be perfect to be useful, and documentation can be incrementally improved in each iteration. For example, if you've drawn a diagram on a whiteboard, it may be good enough to take a photo and put it in the wiki. Only when it needs to be presented to an outside party would it then make sense to recreate it in a diagramming tool such as Visio.

- When investigating and documenting requirements, realize and anticipate that requirements will change, and use simple techniques such as user stories and prioritization backlogs (which we'll examine in Chapter 14).

On the one hand, agile documentation suggests that you write documentation at the last minute. One summarizing guideline has been stated as "Create a document only when the lack of that document begins to cause more pain than the pain of creating the document." On the other hand, there are things that should be decided upon and documented early on in a project because they are difficult to change once the project is underway — in other words, the product's *architecture*. So there is always a balance to be sought. Again, agile approaches do not necessarily mean "no documentation", but rather, "just enough documentation".

Note that in custom development projects, you may have a contractual obligation to deliver specific documentation to your client. In such cases, some agile documentation approaches and techniques may not be suitable.

For more information on lean and lightweight approaches to project documentation, the book *Agile Documentation* (Rüping, 2003) is recommended.

Designing a documentation portfolio

At the beginning of your project, you will need to decide on how designers will communicate designs to the developers and testers. Your project's **documentation portfolio** is simply a list of the different types of documentation artifacts and prototypes that you expect to generate during your project. Naturally, this is never set in stone — if something is not working well, then you can explore alternatives and make changes — but it is always helpful when starting a new project to take a few moments to think through which techniques and artifacts you will use.

Here are some suggestions for user interface-related documentation artifacts that you may wish to consider for your project. We will address most of the throughout the book. Some techniques are suitable for a formal, waterfall-style approach, and other techniques are more likely to be found in agile projects. There is also a great deal of overlap between some of the items, and not all items in this list will be applicable for every kind of product, so consider this list to be a source of ideas rather than a checklist of documents that you must use in your project.

- User Requirements Document (URD)

- Market Requirements Document (MRD)

- Product Requirements Document (PRD)

- Requirements traceability matrix

- Personas

- Usability metrics and targets

- Interaction concept

- Domain models and/or data models

- Glossary

- Navigation map

- Style guide

- Functional specifications

- Technical specifications

- Use cases

- User stories

- High-fidelity prototypes

- Low-fidelity prototypes

- Test plans

- Test cases

- Test data

- Test execution logs

- Bug/defect databases

- User observation logs

- Checklists

- Project plans

End-user documentation deliverables like manuals, tutorials, and help system content are important for a satisfactory user experience. These will be discussed in Chapter 15.

You may wish to create **templates** for each type of document, as these can provide a rudimentary structure to help writers get started, and can ensure some degree of consistency. Overly rigid rules and forms should be avoided, however, as there can be situations where bypassing the prescribed document structure can explain things more clearly.

6

Understanding product requirements

In order to effectively design a software product, you need to understand its requirements. This chapter explains what you information you need to find out about your users and their tasks, shows you how to discover that information, and offers suggestions on recording and communicating your findings.

Requirements

Requirements are statements of the things that your product must achieve for it to be considered successful. If you are building a customized solution for a client, requirements express the wants and needs of your client. If you are building a product for sale to a wider market, requirements express the aggregate wants and needs of potential customers that will be necessary for the product to be able to sell enough copies to be economically successful.

Requirements for software systems are typically classified into two types:

- **Functional requirements** are the features your product will offer — the functions and actions it will support. For example, some functional requirements for a word processor might be that it must support styling text with bold and italic type, it must allow documents to be printed, and it must allow images to be embedded in documents.

- **Non-functional requirements** are quality constraints that are general or "cross-cutting" in nature. Performance, security, stability, reliability, capacity, and scalability are examples. For instance, an e-commerce website might be required to serve 10,000 users concurrently and to serve pages with a response time of 2.0 seconds or less.

The **scope** of your product and project is defined by the set of requirements that need to be implemented. Without careful management, additional wishes and demands will continually be added to the project's scope, and this type of *scope creep* can threaten your ability to deliver on schedule.

Requirements should state the needs of users and customers, without specifying a particular solution for meeting those needs. In other words, requirements should state *what* the product should do, but not *how* it should do it. Defining exactly *how* the product will meet the requirements is the goal of product design.

In a perfectly disciplined, sequential process, requirements would be gathered and documented, and then subsequently, in a separate analysis and design step, a design would be generated for a solution that will meet the requirements. In many projects, though, the activities intentionally take place together in a blended, parallel form; the requirements often aren't recorded and managed formally, and the team jumps straight into product design.

The idealized, sequential process also isn't fully realistic, because it's virtually impossible to get the requirements right the first time, and requirements often tend to change throughout the life of a software project. Introducing iterative and ongoing requirements analysis is recommended so that requirements change can be more easily managed, and so that the team's understanding of the needs of customers and users can be continually improved.

It should be possible to verify whether the product meets the stated requirements. Some high-level requirements, such as "The product shall be easy to learn and use", can be of such a subjective nature that is not objectively possible to test or prove that the product fulfils the requirement. For such requirements, it is important to state **acceptance criteria** that are stated in concrete, measurable terms. So for "The product shall be easy to learn and use", a measurable acceptance criterion might be "95 percent of users will be able to successfully process a standard passport application after the two-day training session".

Some requirements are "definitional"; they result from, and form part of, your definition of what the purpose and market positioning of your product is. But most requirements exist to ensure that the needs and interests of users and other *stakeholders* are satisfied by your product. Let's now take a closer look at who stakeholders are.

Stakeholders

Stakeholders are all of the different people, groups, and organizations that are affected by the success or failure of the project.

Your product will be operated by users, and your focus should be on designing the product to meet the wants and needs of the users. But in reality, you also have to satisfy other stakeholders, both within and outside your organization. These stakeholders will often contribute requirements and impose constraints, which may conflict with the requirements that are more directly relevant to the needs of the users.

Designing your product can often become a balancing act of trade-offs and compromises that are economic or political in nature. For example, you may wish to create a product with an enormous feature set, but the project manager and project sponsor will not permit this, as it would cause the project to exceed the deadline and budget constraints. Or the company president may insist that the product be decorated with bright neon pink and green branding, and because the president holds the power, you have little influence.

Understanding who the relevant stakeholders are in your project is a good first step to eliciting and managing requirements. Examples of stakeholders that you might encounter are:

- The **project sponsor**, usually a senior executive or an entrepreneur who initiates a project and makes available the funding and resources. The sponsor will tend to work to protect the project from competing forces and agendas in the organization.

- The **project manager** usually reports to the project sponsor and is responsible for planning the project and seeing it through to successful completion.

- Team members in the project.

- Other managers, departments, and specialists that you must interact with in your organization (e.g., marketing department, legal department).

- Government bodies and regulatory authorities that create legislation and rules that must be complied with.

- The **client**, for a custom development project, or **customers**, for products sold to a market.

- **End users**, the people who will be actually operating your product.

- **Secondary users**, discussed below.

Users vs. buyers/customers

For most consumer products, the user has purchased the product for their own personal use, and so the user is the customer.

But for many products, the end user and the buyer or customer are not always the same. End users use the product in a hands-on manner on a day-to-day basis. The customer is the person who makes the final decision to purchase the product.

For enterprise software such as enterprise resource planning (ERP) systems, high-level company executives will make the decision to purchase the system, but possibly may never operate the software themselves. Similarly, young children may influence purchasing decisions for educational computer games, but it is the parents or other adults who will actually buy the product. Products purchased as gifts are another example of where the customer is not the end user.

So while user experience design and usability testing must focus on the needs of the end users, if your users and customers are separate groups, your product must also simultaneously appeal to the people who will actually buy it.

Secondary users

Some products are used by staff members of an organization who use the product to carry out work in order to serve the organization's customers. The staff members are the end users or **primary users** of the product, and the customers whom the end users serve are called **secondary users**.

Imagine the case of financial aid advisors at a college who use a software system to process student loan applications. Students speak with the advisors but do not use the software directly. The advisors are the primary or end users of the system, while the students are the secondary users.

While secondary users do not use a system directly, they are impacted by it, and a system that leads to poor service delivery to the secondary users cannot be considered successful.

Eliciting requirements from stakeholders

Once you know who your stakeholders are, you can then work towards understanding what they expect and need from the project and the product.

Interviewing stakeholders is the most common and most effective technique. Interviews may be **structured**, following a pre-prepared list of questions, or may be more **free-flowing**, allowing the interviewer to adjust the flow of the conversation to delve deeper and obtain further information when interesting or unexpected issues and opinions are expressed.

Questionnaire surveys offer the chance to collect responses from a large group, but restrict the feedback to a set list of questions with limited opportunities to probe into individuals' particular concerns and ideas. Surveys can be useful for validating your assumptions, however; you can determine what percentage of the stakeholders say they desire or would use various features.

For the end users who will actually use the product, the technique of **user observation** — watching users as they go about performing their tasks, and asking questions about *why* they do the things the way they do — is extremely valuable. During an observation session, the user may be performing a manual task that will be automated by your product, or the user may be operating a prototype of your product, an older version of your product, or a competing product.

In user observation sessions, you may consider using the **think-aloud protocol** technique, in which you ask the users to vocalize their thoughts and explain what they is doing at each step. While this can provide valuable insights, it can disrupt the flow of work, as many users find it difficult and unnatural to do, and users can feel embarrassed if they make a mistake while being so closely monitored.

Analytics, the collection and analysis of data such as **usage logs** and **usage statistics,** can be provide useful insights into how existing products are being used, including what features are being used most frequently, and where users are running into problems. This can help identify and prioritize requirements.

Requirements elicitation can also be aided with **research and analysis of source material** such as relevant books, academic literature, white papers, market research reports, and so on. If your project involves creating a new version of an existing product, inspecting past project documentation such as specifications, test results, and reports can provide a large source of material; this is sometimes called **documentation archaeology**.

You do need to be careful not to rely too heavily on past documents and repeat mistakes if the past projects were not deemed to be successful.

For the purposes of designing usable interfaces, of course, the most important stakeholders to consider are the end users of the product. Let's now examine how to understand your users' characteristics.

Understanding your users

You will want to find out characteristics of your end users (who we'll just call *users* from here on) and the work they will do with your product.

While every user is a unique individual, users will share common characteristics, and these commonalities are often most pronounced for role-related subgroupings.

User segments and roles

Many products can be used by different groups or categories of users. These groups, or **user segments**, have different goals and reasons for using the product, and in some cases the groups have distinct demographics.

Websites and software use **roles** to restrict access to functionality to different user segments. For instance, a web-based discussion forum will assign most users a "contributor" role, which permits posting and replying to messages, but some trusted users will be assigned the "moderator" role, enabling them to additionally edit and delete messages and ban problematic contributors from participating.

Other products may be general-purpose tools that can be used for various purposes, or may offer a wealth of features that users may use in various combinations. These products don't have explicit roles. For example, word processors may be used to write letters, business documents, essays, reports, novels, technical books, journalism articles, diary entries, webpages, and so on, and the needs of users for each case could be different. You'd also expect a word processor to be used by a very diverse user community — students, professionals, and home users, with varying ranges of educational attainment, and in some cases, with various physical impairments. User segments could be created based on these different groups, or based on the different uses of the product.

Understanding what user segments and roles are relevant for your product is an important early step, as the requirements of users in each group will drive the design of your product.

User characteristics

Once you have made an initial list of user segments or roles for your product, your next step is to understand the general characteristics of users in each group.

The following is a list of some of the characteristics you might want to know about each user segment. Not all characteristics are relevant for all types of product — some may only be appropriate for software used at a workplace, for instance.

- Age
- Gender
- Educational background
- Language and culture
- Computing skills
- Physical abilities and disabilities
- Domain-related knowledge and skills (e.g., accounting knowledge for an accounting application)
- Job experience and competence
- Place in the organizational hierarchy
- Attitudes, motivation, and morale
- Persistence, patience, confidence, problem-solving ability, curiosity, ability to deal with change, etc.
- Frustrations and problems relating to the user's tasks or activities
- General sources of stress or anxiety (e.g., deadlines, performance targets, workplace competition)

Additionally, you may also give some though to the context in which your users will use your product:

- The physical environment (e.g., home, office, factory, vehicle, oil rig, on-the-go in an urban environment, etc.)
- The social environment (position within organization, relationship to other groups, political and interpersonal factors, degree of freedom, influence in decision-making, etc.)

Since every individual is unique, there is a risk of creating generalized stereotypes that doesn't accurately describe many users in a user segment. So for some characteristics, you might describe an approximate range and an average. For instance, bank tellers at a particular financial institution might happen to range in age from 20 to 50 years of age, with the average age being 28.

For each user segment or role, you may want to write up the characteristics as a brief **profile**, which can then be reviewed and discussed with your project team. A profile for a user segment can be presented simply as a list with relevant characteristics described in point form. You might use a matrix to compare user segments side-by-side. Alternatively, you can represent user segments by means of *personas*.

Personas

Personas are a modelling technique introduced and popularized by Alan Cooper.

A **persona** or **user persona** is a brief textual description of a fictional character who is representative of a stereotypical user in a user segment. The persona describes some invented personal details about the character, explains in general terms what they do with the product, discusses the context or environment in which they use the product, and mentions some of the problems, frustrations, and concerns that they might face.

You should invent a fictional name and a descriptive title for each persona; for example, Carol Jones, an insurance adjuster, or Bob Davis, a middle-aged man wishing to book a vacation for his family. To make the persona more tangible and memorable, it's common to write a paragraph or so with a narrative of the person's background or history, and you might even include a photograph, perhaps selected from a stock photo repository.

For example, a sample persona for a new word processing product might be as follows:

> **Persona: Alice Smith, aspiring first-time novelist**
>
> *Alice is 32 years old, divorced, and has a two-year-old daughter. She has a bachelor's degree in English Literature from a state university, and currently works full-time as a marketing assistant for a major pharmaceutical firm. Alice sees herself as a very artistic person, and dislikes the fact that her corporate job offers no real opportunities to express herself creatively. She is particularly passionate about reading historical fiction, and so she now wishes to pursue her long-time dream of writing her own novel in this genre.*

Because of her job and child-care responsibilities, Alice tries to get her writing done in small blocks either early in the morning, or late in the evening after she has put her daughter to bed. On weekends, she enjoys writing while sitting in her favorite coffee shop. She is frustrated that it takes her a lot of time to get warmed up and get into the "flow" of writing, and because she only has short windows of time to work on her book, she doesn't feel that she is making very good progress.

Alice is currently using Microsoft Word on her MacBook laptop, but she is finding it difficult to organize her notes, plan out her plot structure, and generate an outline. She has character and plot notes and multiple chapters spread across multiple Word documents, as well as hand-written notes in a notebook and on various loose scraps of paper, and switching between these is becoming a hassle. She feels she could be more productive if she could just get a better handle on organizing all of her project materials.

She would like to have her novel published by a big-name publisher, but she knows that this is difficult for a first-time fiction author. She is considering self-publishing, but has not had an opportunity to research what is involved, and she is particularly worried about the costs involved. She would also like to make her novel available on e-book readers like the Kindle, but she is unsure of how to convert her manuscript to an e-book format and get it listed on major booksellers' sites like Amazon.com.

The advantage of personas is that they help your team develop a shared understanding of the requirements of each user segment, and they encourage empathy with the end users of your product. By bringing to life someone from each user segment, with a human name and face, designers can design specifically with that particular user in mind. When designing a task flow or a screen, you might ask, "How would Alice want this information presented?" or "How would Alice react in this situation?"

Personas can also help focus usability tests and evaluations. For preliminary evaluations of a prototype, tests could be carried out by somebody pretending to act in the role of the persona, or at least with that persona in mind. (Of course, it is preferable to involve real users from the user segments.)

You can also use the personas to prioritize the functional requirements. For instance, one release could concentrate on the core features needed by the Alice persona, and then the next release could concentrate on another persona.

Personas are not without criticism; many people find the invention of fictional names and personal details to be highly gimmicky. Trying to represent a diverse user segment with a single persona runs the risk that the persona doesn't accurately represent a large percentage of the members of the user segment. And if you try to write up personas without ever actually speaking to real live users, these completely hypothetical personas may have no relation to reality.

From user characteristics to requirements

User characteristics are not requirements, but characteristics can serve as a source of requirements.

For example, if your user community is distributed around the world, and your users prefer to, or must, use their native languages rather than English, then you can establish a requirement that the product be available in various localized forms for different countries and languages. Or if your user community includes people with mild visual impairment (they need to wear glasses), you will likely want to have a requirement for the ability to adjust the font size.

Understanding the work and tasks

Software exists to get things done, and the things that users want to get done we will call **work**.

Work is a suitable term for the activities that users carry out with productivity applications, where the goal is to produce a deliverable of value, such as an essay, a financial statement, or a poster. It is also suitable when referring to business systems that users operate to provide services to customers or to manage and administer the organization.

Of course, there is a vast category of entertainment and communications software where the activities, like watching cat videos, shooting alien invaders, or flirting, revolve around recreation and socializing rather than producing something of commercial, intellectual, or artistic value. For the purposes of this book, however, we'll still refer to the activity that users do with the software as "work".

Work exists in a particular **domain** and **context**. Banking software, for example, obviously deals with the domain of banking, where concepts like accounts, transactions, loans, interest, and fees are relevant. And banking software is used in the context of a specific organization — in this case, a particular bank. So the work that users (bank tellers, loan officers, and so on in this case) do with banking software thus involves users working with the domain objects in the context of serving customers to further the organizational aims of the bank.

The process of designing your software product, then, usually revolves largely around understanding the domain and the work, choosing what parts of the work your product will support, and then specifically designing how your product will help the user carry out that work.

Users' work often consists of multiple **tasks**. In some applications, tasks can be highly structured, with a defined sequence of actions. For example, registering a new member into a medical insurance plan would have a very formally defined workflow. In other applications, tasks are more fluid, and users may have many things on the go at once. For example, while retouching a photo, a user may use various drawing tools and switch between them frequently while working towards the vague goal of making the photograph look more attractive.

Different user segments will typically engage in different kinds of work, so some tasks will only be relevant for certain user roles. There may be many tasks shared between roles, and sometimes tasks may be used by different user segments to achieve different ends.

When analyzing and designing the work and tasks relevant for your product, some questions to keep in mind include:

- How do users do the task currently? Do they use a competing product in the same category? Do they use a different type of product or some combination of products? Do they currently lack a technology-based solution?

- What are users' biggest complaints about the way they currently do the task? What are the biggest problems for them (or for their organization, in a work context)? What are the biggest time sinks, the major causes of errors, the sources of frustration?

- Are there any laws or regulations that dictate how the task is to be done (e.g., safety rules, the tax code, Generally Accepted Accounting Principles, etc.)?

The work and tasks will give rise to a large number of functional requirements for what features the product must offer and how the features should work. (In Chapter 14, we'll revisit the topics of understanding and modelling work and take a closer look at designing and documenting task flows and interactions.)

Because work is intricately linked with the application's problem domain, a critical part of understanding and modelling the work and tasks involves understanding and modelling the domain and the data your application will deal with. We'll examine this in Chapter 7.

Documenting requirements

On the basis of the information you've gathered about your users, the domain, and the work and tasks, you'll want to begin recording requirements for your product.

For each requirement, you will typically want to record the following information, at the minimum:

- A unique requirement ID number or code, for ease of reference

- A "headline" or summary description of the requirement

- A more detailed description, if necessary

- Acceptance criteria, i.e., some specific test or measurement that can be done to verify that the requirement has been fulfilled

- The role(s) for which the requirement is applicable

- Dependencies or relationships between this requirement and other requirements

You'll also usually want to have some way of indicating the prioritization, and you'll typically need some form of categorization scheme. You may or may not wish to record project management information, such as an estimate of the work involved, target milestones or deadlines, and so on.

For purposes of traceability, you will likely also want to indicate who created the requirement, and the date the requirement was created and/or approved (and ideally, you'd want to be able to track the version history of changes to the requirement, if possible).

It is recommended that you create a template so that all of your requirements include the same information items. An example of a requirement recorded using a template is shown in Figure 6-1.

Requirement ID	65
Summary description	The system shall allow a customer's annual statement to be generated for the current year or any past year on record.
Detailed description	The statement shall include all transactions during the chosen calendar year, and shall include the final balance at the end of the year (or the current balance if the current year has been selected).
	The generation of the report can be triggered by the customer via a function in the web portal. It can also be generated by a customer service representative or manager.
Acceptance criteria	The generated report contains the appropriate and correct data and content.
	The report's appearance adheres to the corporate visual design and branding standards.
	The report is generated in one of the acceptable file formats defined in the project handbook.
Requirement type	Functional
Category	Reporting - Customer Accounts
Priority	Medium
Implementation estimate	5 person-days
Depends on	15, 24, 25, 56, 59
See also	80
Created by	Alice Smith
Created on	09.09.2013
Approval status	Pending review

FIGURE 6-1

Some teams like to write requirements on paper cards. This is an excellent way to get started when brainstorming and discussing requirements, but of course this tends to become unmanageable in the long term for non-trivial projects. Requirements are often recorded in a spreadsheet, or in a word processing document with a template form that can be duplicated and filled out. There are also specialized requirements management tools available, and many companies and teams have been known to create their own requirements database.

The book *Mastering the Requirements Process* (Robertson and Robertson, 2012) recommends that all requirements pass through a so-called **quality gateway** process before being accepted as being part of the scope of the project. To pass the quality gateway, each requirement is inspected with a basic checklist that tests for completeness, and an authority (such as the project manager, product manager, or a review committee) must formally approve the requirement. This review process should also involve checking for conflicts and contradictions amongst the requirements, so that such issues can be resolved sooner rather than later.

To document in detail how it is intended that the user will interact with the product, and how the product will behave, design techniques like *use cases* are often used in addition to requirements. We'll explore this further in Chapter 14.

User stories

A list of potentially thousands of requirements of the form "The system shall..." makes it hard for readers to get an overall understanding of what the product is intended to do. In the agile community, informal **user stories** are often preferred over formal requirements templates.

User stories are intended to be concise and informal, and serve primarily as a basis for discussion, rather than attempting to capture all possible details related to the requirement.

User stories take the form of a simple statement that states a *goal* of a user, and then gives the *rationale* for why the user would want to achieve that goal.

A user story is a brief summary statement that usually follows the pattern:

> *"As a <role>, I want to <description of function> so that <rationale>."*

This pattern manages to capture "who" (the role), "what" (the function), and "why" (the rationale, i.e., the benefit or justification).

You could omit the rationale clause in cases where it is self-evident, but it is often useful to understand the reason why some piece of functionality should be included in the system, so don't make it a habit to omit it.

Here are some examples of user stories:

- *"As a mobile phone subscriber, I want to be able to block calls from a specific telephone number so that I do not have to be interrupted by repeated nuisance phone calls from telemarketers."*

- *"As a system administrator, I want to be able to create new user accounts so that new hires can access the system."*

- *"As a manager, I want to be able to view the timesheet records of my direct reports so that I can verify that staff are working on relevant tasks and billing appropriately."*

User stories can capture functionality at various levels of detail and abstraction. A high-level user story that encapsulates a very large amount of functionality is called an **epic**, and can be broken down into more detailed user stories.

We should note that non-functional requirements can also be captured as user stories. For instance:

- *"As a user, I want the system's webpages to load in under two seconds so that I can maintain a steady work rhythm without having to stop and wait."*

User stories are intended to be short; the general guideline is that a user story should be able to be written on an index card. But user stories may be accompanied by a more detailed description, sometimes called a "conversation", when more details are required.

User stories should eventually be accompanied by acceptance criteria, such as a test procedure that can be performed to verify that the user story has been implemented as described.

User stories and project management

When used for project planning purposes, user stories should also include an estimates of the amount of work involved for implementation. While the estimate can be stated in person-days, the usual recommendation is to use **story points**, which are an arbitrary measure of relative complexity, effort, and risk. You define your own story points scale by choosing a relatively trivial user story to count as the base unit, worth one story point. If you then rate another user story as being worth 20 story points, then it indicates that the complexity, effort, and risk are such that, on the average, it will take approximately 20 times as long as the base user story to complete.

In the Scrum methodology, user stories are placed on a list called the **product backlog**. The product backlog can include user stories that are wished for, but which may never actually get implemented. At the beginning of each iteration, or **sprint**, the priorities of all of the user stories are reevaluated, and a set of user stories are selected on the basis of priority and estimates to form the **sprint backlog**, representing the work scheduled to be done in the sprint.

Writing requirements for usability

As discussed briefly earlier, we often find ourselves writing usability requirements such as "The product shall be easy to use" or "The product shall be easy to learn". The problem with these requirements is that they are *qualitative, subjective* statements that express general goals, and it is impossible to objectively prove that the product fulfils these requirements. Different evaluators will have different subjective opinions on whether the product actually is easy to use and learn.

Acceptance criteria for such requirements should be stated in terms of **usability metrics,** which are *quantitative* performance measurements of some usability-related factor. The process of finding quantitative, measurable proxy indicators for a qualitative concept or phenomenon is called **operationalization**.

For example, we can take the requirement "The product shall be easy to use" and operationalize it with acceptance criteria such as:

- *"An average trained user shall be able to process a standard application form containing no special cases in under five minutes."*

- *"An average user shall not have to access the online help system more than twice per hour under normal operating conditions."*

- *"An average user shall report no more than five annoyances per hour of system operation."*

Usability metrics

Tyldesley (1988), who summarizes material from Whiteside *et al.* (1998), suggests the following factors that could used in formulating usability metrics:

1. Time to complete a task

2. Percentage of task completed

3. Percentage of task completed per unit time (speed metric)

4. Ratio of successes to failures

5. Time spent on errors

6. Percentage or number of errors

7. Percentage or number of competitors that do some particular aspect better than the current product

8. Number of commands used

9. Frequency of help or documentation use

10. Time spent using help or documentation

11. Percentage of favorable to unfavorable user commands

12. Number of repetitions of failed commands

13. Number of runs of successes and of failures

14. Number of times the interface misleads the user

15. Number of good and bad factors recalled by users

16. Number of available commands not invoked

17. Number of regressive behaviors

18. Number of users preferring your product

19. Number of times users need to work around a problem

20. Number of times the user is disrupted from a work task

21. Number of times the user loses control of the system

22. Number of times the user expresses frustration or satisfaction

You can also ask evaluators to judge usability, learnability, satisfaction, or other subjective factors using a rating scale. Statistical derivations such as average values can then serve as a form of measurement. There are reliability issues such as bias that can threaten the validity of the results, so you do need to be careful when drawing conclusions from such data.

7

Understanding and modelling the domain and data

All software manipulates information or data in some way, and to be able to design a user interface for a product, you need to understand the information and data that the product will present and manipulate, and how it is structured.

Many types of projects don't have particularly strict requirements, and in these projects, a top-down approach to design works well: The user interface designer sketches out designs for how the application should look and work, and from these designs, the technical architects and developers proceed to figure out the data structures needed to support it. Games would be the best example of products that can be designed with this approach.

On the other hand, imagine you've been hired to design the user interface for an income tax preparation software package. You can't just make up whatever you want out of thin air like a game designer could; to calculate the taxes correctly according to the law, you must compel the user to enter specific financial information. And so as a user interface designer in such a project, you would have flexibility in terms of how you will design the look-and-feel of the application, and you would decide how to break up all the information the user must enter into different screens or forms, and then you would design the layout and behavior of each of those screens or forms. But you would be constrained by requirements to include certain fields such as "Taxable Income from Employment" on those forms, or else your application would not calculate the correct tax amounts and would thus violate certification standards for tax software, making the product unsalable.

So in projects involving highly structured, data-driven systems with strict requirements, design in practice often tends to follow more of a bottom-up approach. The structure of the data needs to be determined before the user interface can be designed, because the user interface is centered around presenting that data and allowing the user to interact with it, and you need to know what that data is before you can design a screen to show it. However, don't interpret this to mean that a perfect and complete understanding of the structure of the data must be finalized before user interface design can begin. In reality, both the understanding of the data and the design of the user interface will change and co-evolve together during the course of a typical project.

In most business system projects, a *domain model* or *data model* is created to describe what pieces of data need to be known and managed by the system, and how those pieces of data are interrelated.

- A **domain model** is a high-level, technology-neutral description of relevant general concepts and entities in the application's domain; for example, banking software deals with the domain of banking, and so accounts, interest, deposits, withdrawals, loans, credit cards, and fees are examples of things in that domain.

- A **data model** is a description of all of the relevant entities, attributes, and relationships that the software must manage, with this description taking into consideration the technical aspects of storing the data (whether it may be in a database, or in files, or some other storage scheme). A data model is detailed enough to make the model directly translatable into a software representation.

This is not a book on data modelling or requirements engineering, but to be an effective user interface designer in many types of projects, you need to be able to at least read and understand a data model, if not create one yourself. And because many user interface designers come from non-programming backgrounds and thus may not be familiar with data models, it's worthwhile taking a look at an example of a data model to get a feel for what's involved.

There are various ways to present a data model, and visual, diagrammatic systems of notation are most popular, though one need not necessarily use visual diagrams to document a data model. A long-standing visual diagramming notation is the **Entity-Relationship Diagram (ERD)**, which is popular in systems that are based around a relational database system.

While ERDs are still very common, most large software development projects now use **object-oriented programming (OOP)** techniques, and the **Unified Modelling Language (UML)**, which is designed for use with the object-oriented methodology, is now considered the de-facto standard visual modelling language for software developers. The UML 2.0 standard defines 14 types of diagrams. One of these, the UML **class diagram**, is similar to the Entity-Relationship Diagram, but has additional features that make it more expressive for representing real-world situations.

Let's take a brief tour of some of the key aspects of object-oriented modelling using UML class diagrams. (If you are an experienced object-oriented designer or developer, you may wish to skip the next section.)

A brief introduction to UML class diagrams

A UML class diagram can represent *entities* (*classes*), *attributes*, *operations*, and various types of *relationships* between entities. Let's explore what each of these terms means by examining the following simplistic UML class diagram showing part of the data model for a banking application:

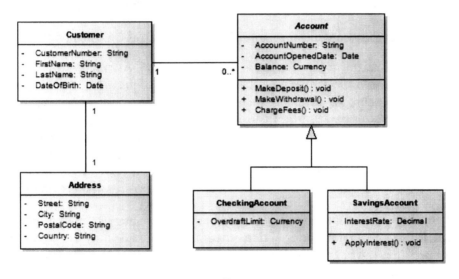

FIGURE 7-1

The boxes represent the various *entities* that the product needs to know about. (When we are talking about things in the domain, we usually use the term *entities*, but when these entities are implemented in software, they are more frequently called *classes*. We'll use the term *entities* here for clarity.) An **entity** represents a thing or a concept, or a set of similar things or concepts, and defines what information is needed to represent an instance of that thing or concept in software. Entities basically represent *nouns* in your domain.

So in Figure 7-1, the Customer entity represents the collection of all of the individual pieces of information, or **attributes**, that our application needs to know about each customer: their customer number, their first and last names, and their date of birth.

The entity is an abstract representation of the idea or concept of an actual thing, much like a blueprint is an abstract representation of a building to be constructed. Once your system is up and running, there will usually be many concrete **instances** of each entity known by the system. (Instances are also known as **instantiations, records,** or **objects**.)

Each instance represents a specific real-world case of the corresponding entity — so for the Customer entity, there might be 500 instances, representing 500 different real customers. Each Customer instance will have its own separate set of values for each attribute, meaning each instance will have its own values for the customer number, name, and so on. One Customer instance might be for a customer with a customer number of 1234567, first name John, last name Smith, and date of birth 05.05.1965. Another Customer instance might be for customer number 2345678, Alice Jones, born 07.07.1977.

In UML class diagrams, the box for an entity is divided into multiple sections:

- The top compartment contains the name of the entity, such as Customer.

- The middle compartment lists the *attributes* for the entity. **Attributes** are the individual data items or fields that describe the properties of the entity. So if the entity represents a noun, the attributes might be thought of as *adjectives* that describe the noun. For the Customer entity, the attributes are CustomerNumber, FirstName, LastName, and DateOfBirth. In domain models, usually just the attribute names are given; for data models suitable for implementation in software, the data type for each attribute is usually given as well. Here, "String" means text, "Date" means a calendar date, and so on.

- The bottom compartment of the box is optional and is frequently omitted. When present, it lists any **operations** or **actions** that instances of an entity can perform. These operations can be thought of as *verbs* that the instance can do. Not all entities will have operations, and operations are typically listed only in data models and not in domain models. (The notation used for naming the operations usually reflects the programming language being used in the system, which is why the example diagram here includes the additional brackets and the "void" annotation.)

Relationships

Relationships between entity classes are represented with lines drawn between boxes. The UML standard uses various styles and combinations of lines and arrows to indicate different types of relationships. Let's examine the two most common relationship types: *associations* and *inheritance*.

Association relationships

The most common type of relationship between entities is the **association**, which we can indicate by drawing a plain line between two boxes. An association relationship means that two specific entity instances (or objects) are linked together in some logical way. In our example diagram above, Customer instances can be linked with Address instances, as well as Account instances.

The numbers alongside a relationship line indicate what is called the **cardinality** of the relationship.

In the sample diagram, the association between Customer and Address shows the number 1 on each side. This is what is called a **1-to-1 relationship**, and this means that every Customer instance must always be linked to exactly one Address instance. In other words, a Customer cannot have more than one address, nor can a Customer exist who doesn't have an address on file; every Customer must always be linked to an Address. And likewise, an Address instance cannot exist in the system if it is not linked to a Customer instance, and an Address instance can only be linked with one specific Customer; no more, and no fewer.

This particular model diagram doesn't allow two customers — let's say, a husband and wife — who happen to live at the same postal address to share one Address record in the system; each Customer must have its own Address, which means there would be data duplication. Two Address records would hold identical postal address data. This particular design may have usability consequences. For example, in this scenario, if the couple moves to a new address, and the wife notifies the bank of her new address, the wife's Customer record will have its associated Address record updated. But because the Address record is not shared by the two customers, the husband's Address record, which is a separate record, will remain unchanged (unless a bank employee figures out the situation and manually changes the record).

The association between Customer and Account, on the other hand, is an example of what is generally called a **1-to-many** relationship. There is a cardinality indicator of 1 on the one side, and the other side, the 0..* notation is shorthand for "zero to many".

This means that the number of Account instances that a Customer can be linked to can be any number between "zero" and "many". So a customer in the system might have no accounts at all, or one, or two, or even fifty accounts.

But the 1 on the other end of the association means that an Account can only belong to one Customer; two Customers cannot share an Account (at least according to this particular data model).

Inheritance (specialization/generalization) relationships

Another type of relationship is the **inheritance** relationship, drawn with a plain line with an open triangular arrowhead at one end.

If you see an inheritance relationship where the arrowhead points from, say, entity Car to entity Vehicle, it indicates that a Car is a specialized kind of Vehicle. In terms of entities, we say that the Car entity **inherits** all of the attributes, operations, and relationships of the Vehicle entity. Car instances have all of the properties defined in the Vehicle entity, but can have additional properties that are specific only to Cars.

We can say that Car is a **subclass**, **subentity**, **specialization**, **specialized type**, or **subtype** of Vehicle. And if the Vehicle entity had multiple subclasses, like Car, Bus, Tank, Bicycle, and JetAircraft, then we would say that Vehicle is the **generalization** of these subclasses, as it represents all of the commonalities shared by those subclasses.

In our banking example in Figure 7-1 above, we will notice that there is an inheritance relationship. There is an entity called Account, and below it, there are two entities, CheckingAccount and SavingsAccount, which are specialized types of Account.

Instances of the CheckingAccount entity take on all of the attributes and operations of Account, and additionally have additional attributes and operations specific to CheckingAccount. So a CheckingAccount instance has the attributes AccountNumber, AccountOpenedDate, Balance, and OverdraftLimit, and can perform the operations MakeDeposit, MakeWithdrawal, and ChargeFees. Likewise, a SavingsAccount instance has the attributes AccountNumber, AccountOpenedDate, Balance, and InterestRate, and can perform the operations MakeDeposit, MakeWithdrawal, ChargeFees, and ApplyInterest.

When a customer opens a checking account at the bank, the software will record this fact by creating a link between the appropriate Customer instance and a new CheckingAccount instance. And when a customer opens a savings account, a link will be made between the Customer instance and a new SavingsAccount instance. Because a Customer can have between "zero" and "many" accounts, a Customer may be linked to any number of CheckingAccounts and any number of SavingsAccounts, or none at all.

But a Customer will never actually be linked to an instance of Account. Why? Account is what we call an **abstract supertype** — which means that no instances of that entity can actually be created in the system. You can only create instances of the subtypes. So if a customer wants to open a new account, he or she must choose a CheckingAccount and/or a SavingsAccount, as no "general" Account can be created.

If you look closely, you will see in the diagram that the entity name "Account" is italicized. This italicization is the convention used in UML for marking an entity as abstract, or *non-instantiable*. Because this is so subtle visually, the notation "<>" is often added inside the top compartment of the box to bring more attention to the fact.

While this brief introduction to UML class diagrams only scratches the surface, it will hopefully get you started if you haven't encountered data models before. If you want to learn more about UML, a web search will uncover plenty of useful resources.

Interpreting data models for user interface design

Why are we discussing data models and why are they important in many projects?

First of all, the data model tells you what entities exist, and what attributes are present for each entity. So if you are designing a form or a screen for editing a customer's address, the data model tells you what fields you have to work with.

Likewise, the relationships between the entities are important for user interface designers to know, because these associations reveal how all the various pieces of data are related. This is important because your application's interface generally cannot be designed in such a way that would violate the relationships in the model. So if your data model allows customers to have multiple accounts, then you need to design the product to allow the user a way to view and access all of the accounts, and functions may be needed for adding and removing accounts. This means that the product will look and behave differently than it would if customers were only permitted to have a single account.

Changing a data model to better fit the real world

You might say that some of the rules we examined in the banking data model example in Figure 7-1 are not very practical for a real bank — two spouses should be able to share a joint account, for instance. And that's correct — this is a highly oversimplified data model.

If you're working with a data model that has been designed by somebody else, it's often inevitable that you will come to some disagreement over how the entities and relationships have been designed. In our bank example, you might argue that customers should be able to have multiple addresses on file, such as a work address as well as a home address. Or you might want the system to keep track of all of the address changes in the past. Or you might want address records to be shared by multiple customers in the same household, so that a change-of-address need only be done once, and the new address becomes effective for all of the customers sharing the address record.

If the design of a data model is hindering your ability to design a usable interface, because the designer's data model doesn't quite match the way your users want or expect things to be, then you should propose changes to the data model and discuss them with your project team.

However, developers and project managers will be resistant to changing the data model, especially if a system is already in use and contains "live" data, because many types of changes can involve a lot of work and expense, and can necessitate data conversion or migration efforts. Data model changes are much easier to accommodate in the earlier stages of a software project.

Usability concerns in moving from a data model to screen designs

When a data model has been created before the screen designs, there is often a temptation to base screen designs off of data models in a direct, "one-to-one" fashion. In fact, software development tools exist that can translate data models or database schemas into rudimentary user interfaces.

While the idea of automatically generating a user interface sounds convenient from a technical standpoint, and initially sounds like a time and money saver, the approach is rarely safe from a usability standpoint. In effect, this can often expose aspects of the implementation model directly to the user, and technical details can be presented that don't match the user's expected conceptual model. (We'll discuss mental models, implementation models, and conceptual models in Chapter 9.)

A mechanical screen generation approach will typically translate each entity into a separate screen, window, or tab. This is not always convenient, and can require the user to navigate excessively. Sometimes there may be fields that logically make sense by being positioned close to each other on the screen, but the fields may actually be stored in attributes in different entities in the model.

Additionally, many tasks in data-driven applications cause **object graphs**, i.e., networks of instances, to be created. For example, with our banking example, if a new customer entered the bank and wanted to open a new account, then a Customer record, an Address record, and one of the Account records would need to be created and interlinked properly. The degree to which the internal representation is exposed to the user can have an enormous impact on usability.

With the mechanical approach, the user would have to know how to add a new Customer record, then add a new Address record, establish the proper link between the Customer and Address record, and then add a new Account record, and link it properly with the Customer record. The user would be responsible for manually generating the object graph with the correct structure, which would require the user to attain a deep knowledge of the internal workings of the software.

Most applications benefit from a task-oriented design approach rather than a purely data-oriented approach. And so in this case, a preferable approach would be to have a function or workflow task that guides the user through a linear process of entering the customer information and address and choosing an account type. The software would then ensure that the records are created and linked according to the proper structure, hiding the internal representation details, and ensuring that no errors are made in this representation that could lead to problems later.

In summary, while designers will often desire to design the user interface first, and then create the data model to support it, this is not always possible in many kinds of software projects, and in many cases, creating the data model first can help aid and structure thinking about how to present information in the user interface. When working from a data model, let the model inform you of what entities and attributes you have to work with, but then design the screens in the way that makes the most logical sense. Think about the tasks that the users have to do, and design task flows that guide users through the work with a minimum of memorization, and without forcing users to know the structure of the data model. Focus on designing a user-friendly experience first, and then map the on-screen elements and structures to the data model.

8

User skill levels and skill acquisition

One of the biggest challenges of user interface design is figuring out how to make your software product comprehensible and learnable for beginners, while at the same time not hindering experts from working productively. This chapter explores the range of skill levels of users can possess, examines how skills and competence can change over time, and suggests ways of facilitating skill attainment by users. With this background, we'll be able to better understand human-computer interaction concepts in upcoming chapters.

User skill levels

The general skill levels of people using a software application might be categorized as follows:

- An **evaluator** is someone who is investigating your product, and has not committed to the product yet, but may be considering buying or adopting it. Evaluators try out a product to see what it can do, to determine whether it meets their needs, and to get a general impression of how it works. There is usually no particular pressing goal or task at hand; the user is just exploring and experimenting with the product.

- A **beginner** is someone who is trying to accomplish tasks with the product, but has little or no past experience with it, and thus may not know how to complete the desired tasks. Beginners often have feelings of uncertainty, and gradually learn by exploring, observing, experimenting, and learning from mistakes. Some — but not all — beginners seek out documentation such as tutorial guides, help systems, or reference manuals.

- An **intermediate user** has used the product for some period of time and is generally able to accomplish desired goals and tasks using it. However, the intermediate user may not have explored all of the product's functionality, and may still be uncertain about some tasks; real comfort and "fluency" has not yet been achieved.

  And because some users may only use the product sporadically (for instance, tax preparation software is usually only used once a year), or because some features may be used very infrequently, the user may have forgotten how to do some tasks, despite having successfully performed them in the past. The book *About Face 3* (Cooper *et al.*, 2006) suggests the term **perpetual intermediates** to refer to users who use the application sporadically and never really get the chance to become experts.

- An **expert user** is very confident and has a deep understanding of the domain and the product. An expert can not only complete tasks without difficulty, but is concerned with getting things done as efficiently and quickly as possible. When faced with a new or unexpected situation, an expert can generally reason about how the product works and find a solution or workaround.

- A **power user** is an expert user who has a particular fascination with the product and often enjoys customizing it and stretching its limits.

Factors influencing skill

The above classification might suggest that all users start off as beginners, and, given enough time using an application, progress to higher levels of skill. But of course this is a simplistic view. There are multiple factors and dimensions of competence, including:

- *Domain knowledge:* If your product is an accounting package, for instance, users without a basic understanding of the fundamental concepts and processes of accounting will tend to be puzzled.

- *General skill with computing/technology:* To some degree, you will usually have to assume that your users have the basic skills to operate similar applications on the device or operating system of choice. For instance, you'll probably assume that users know how to operate a mouse or a touchscreen, and are aware of concepts like opening and saving files.

- *General intelligence and reasoning capacity:* When faced with new situations, some people are simply more intellectually curious and more capable of problem-solving than others.

- *Persistence and motivation:* When faced with challenges and unfamiliar circumstances, some people will give up easily, while others will keep trying and experimenting.

Assumptions about minimum skills

In defining your product, you will have to make some basic assumptions about what minimum skills and knowledge you will expect new users to have. If you are producing productivity software for a general audience, for instance, you may decide that it is not your responsibility to train people who don't know how to turn on a computer and operate a mouse. You may simply declare that such people are simply outside of your target market. This is probably a safe assumption today, although it might have been different, say, in the early 1980s, when microcomputers were first gaining mainstream adoption in businesses and homes.

But you have to make sure that your assumptions really match the reality of your marketplace. If you're selling shrink-wrapped accounting software, for example, many of your customers will be first-time small businesspeople with little or no exposure to bookkeeping and accounting. Including a "Getting Started" guidebook or video that introduces just enough concepts and terminology to get started might be what you need to prevent frustrated customers from returning your product to the store.

Familiarity with similar products

If a user has used a similar product before, that familiarity can help in learning your product. In some cases however, it can act as a disadvantage, as the user's expectations and presumptions may conflict with the structure of your product.

Designing for different skill levels

Revisiting the basic classification of user skill levels, what are some guidelines to keep in mind so that the design of your product can meet the needs of each type of user?

- For *evaluators*, the product must give a good first impression. The visual appearance should look appealing and inviting, and should not be overwhelmingly complex.

Demo videos and walk-through tutorials with step-by-step instructions can help users understand the basic functions of the product and try out simple tasks. If applicable, consider providing sample files or documents that the user can open and experiment with in the application.

- For *beginners*, use visual design, information architecture, and interaction design principles to make the product's functionality easily discoverable and learnable (we'll discuss these in depth in upcoming chapters). Offer wizards for setting up projects or to guide the user through complex tasks. Offer undo/redo functions to encourage experimentation and to make it easy to correct mistakes. Offer in-depth tutorials and introductory guides, either as manuals, or as online help content.

- For *intermediate users*, in addition to the above, ensure that the online help is indexed and searchable so that instructions and answers to questions can be easily located. Online discussion forums where users can ask and answer questions are also useful for many kinds of products.

- For *expert users*, ensure that tasks can be completed as quickly and efficiently as possible. Provide shortcut keys, and allow users to bypass wizards and turn off any pop-ups or other aids intended to offer help to beginners.

- *Power users* often want to be able to customize the application, and, if applicable, may expect to be able to write scripts to automate tasks. Online discussion forums are often popular with such users for exchanging tips and tricks.

How users' skills and competence change over time

As users gain experience with using a product, their skills tend to improve in the following ways:

- Increased awareness of the product's capabilities (what it can do)

- Increased knowledge of how to perform tasks, and how to deal with special cases

- Decreased error rate

- Increased productivity, speed, throughput, and efficiency

- Increased confidence

In general, one might also expect the *quality* of the work done to increase as well. But quality is difficult to define and measure. For rote, repetitive, mechanical work, simply getting the work done quickly and with few errors makes it high-quality work, and so more practice will almost always lead to better-quality work. For creative tasks, not only is judging quality a very subjective and inherently unmeasurable affair, but also more practice will not necessarily guarantee better quality work. Skill at a creative endeavor is also generally unrelated to skill at operating a software product: If someone is a bad artist with no visual design sense, learning and becoming competent with Photoshop's features will not necessary make that artist's work more visually appealing.

Practice

The most reliable way to get better at a skill is to *practice* — that is, to repeatedly perform (or rehearse the performance of) a task.

In some situations, practice "just happens", in the sense that users end up doing some activity repeatedly simply because it is a part of their work or daily routine. Card *et al.* (1983, p. 188) observe that "people generally become skilled in whatever becomes routine for them".

But by intentionally practicing with focused attention, having in mind the specific goal of improving one's skill, and challenging oneself to work at increasing levels of difficulty, one can be said to be engaging in **deliberate practice**. Deliberate practice involves carefully monitoring and evaluating one's own work and results, and actively seeking out ways to improve.

As users gain experience with an activity through practice, their performance tends to improve rapidly at first, but then the rate of improvement gradually slows down until a peak performance level is reached. For many manual tasks, a reasonable measure of performance is the average time taken to complete the task, and this measurement tends to follow the pattern of rapid improvement followed by steady but increasingly less rapid improvement. The **Power Law of Practice** is a mathematical description of this effect, verified by psychological experiments, and can be illustrated graphically as shown in Figure 8-1:

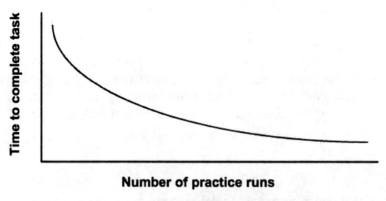

FIGURE 8-1

Many, but not all, performance metrics will tend to follow this phenomenon. The Power Law of Practice applies to most mechanical ("sensory-motor") and cognitive skills, but does not necessarily apply to learning in the sense of knowledge acquisition (Card *et al.*, 1983).

Skills atrophy

Without continual ongoing practice, skills will gradually tend to atrophy and fade over time. In general, motor skills (like riding a bicycle) do not atrophy as quickly as knowledge-based skills (like long division). But atrophied skills can be refreshed and improved again with revision and practice.

It is difficult to predict what knowledge and skills will be retained and what will be forgotten by users. As designers, it is important to recognize that skills atrophy does occur. Complex applications should provide online help systems or other forms of documentation that users can refer to in order to refresh their memories of how to accomplish tasks. To the maximum extent possible, try to structure the system to avoid memorization: guide users through task flows and provide appropriate clues, rather than requiring the memorization of sequences of commands.

Attaining competence

A useful model of how people improve at an activity is the **Four Stages of Competence** model (Robinson, 1974). According to this model, a user goes through the following stages in mastering a skill:

- **Unconscious incompetence**: The user is unaware of how bad he or she is at the skill, or may even be completely unaware that the skill exists at all.

- **Conscious incompetence**: While attempting the skill, the user gradually becomes aware of a deficiency in the skill area, and realizes that improving at the skill will require learning and practicing, which can sometimes be an overwhelming and daunting realization.

- **Conscious competence**: By means of practice, the user becomes able to perform the activity competently, but slowly. Performing the activity requires a lot of concentration, focus, and effort.

- **Unconscious competence**: The user is able to do the activity confidently, effortlessly, naturally, automatically, and quickly without consciously thinking about it. Depending on the skill, the user may even be able to do other things at the same time. The skill has become "second nature".

To better understand these stages, you might try thinking back to your personal experiences of learning to drive an automobile. You probably went through these four stages, and today you are probably so *unconsciously competent* that you can eat or sing along to songs on the radio while driving.

Judging competence

If you are conducting usability studies or questionnaire surveys, you should be aware that people tend to be very poor judges of their own competence. People who are incompetent at a particular activity tend to grossly overestimate their level of skill, while conversely, many experts, often because they are aware of how much they still do not know, tend to underestimate their own level of skill. This phenomenon is known as the **Dunning-Kruger effect**.

Facilitating skills acquisition and development

Instructional materials such as introductory tutorials, videos, reference documentation, and searchable online help systems can offer the guidance users need to get started with your product.

In corporate environments, when a new application is rolled out, users typically take part in training sessions. The effectiveness of such training can vary greatly. In general, simply *telling* someone how to do something is rarely sufficient. *Showing* how to do it is better, and to be truly effective, training has to include repeated *hands-on practice* with real-life situations.

Increasingly, some products are taking a **coaching** approach to helping users figure out how to use them. For instance, in some games, as you play the first level, the game automatically pauses at certain locations to point out what controls to use or what goal needs to be achieved to complete the level. Similarly, some productivity applications and websites use pop-up **callouts** to draw attention to features and controls that may not be immediately obvious.

Feedback is important in learning and making sense of new situations. If the user performs some actions and then sees that the results of those actions matched what he or she intended to do, then the feedback signals that those actions were evidently correct. If it is likely that this sequence of actions will be needed again in the future, the user will try to remember them, but it may also take additional practice with many repetitions before the actions are actually memorized.

Feedback can also take the form of a more explicit acknowledgement of success. For instance, in a game, when the player completes a level or achieves a similar objective, the game will usually pause to reward the achievement with some kind of animation or music. This also provides encouragement to continue playing.

9

The fundamentals of human-computer interaction

To design a software application that is easy to learn and use, it is helpful to understand the basic psychology of human-computer interaction. In this chapter, we'll explore some of the key concepts and learn the practical implications for design.

How users get things done with a software application

Users interact with software by performing physical actions with input devices such as keyboards, mice, touchscreens, and microphones. Graphical user interfaces present controls like buttons, sliders, and drop-down boxes, and the user performs actions on these controls, either directly by gesturing on a touchscreen, or indirectly via mouse clicks or keyboard keystrokes.

Non-graphical interfaces typically rely on the user issuing commands to perform actions, whether by typing them in at a command line, or via spoken commands in a voice-activated system.

But how do users know which actions to perform to get their work done?

The usual model for thinking about this involves a hierarchical breakdown of work into *goals*, *tasks*, and *actions*:

- A user usually has a high-level **goal** in mind of what he or she wishes to accomplish with the application. This might be something like writing a letter, retouching a photograph, conducting a video chat with a coworker, paying a credit card bill, or comparing prices for flights. Goals are statements about *what* the user wants to achieve, rather than *how* it will be achieved.

- To accomplish a goal, the user usually has to perform some number of general steps or structured activities that we could call **tasks**.

- To perform a task, the user will perform *actions* in the interface. **Actions** are specific operations involving the user interface, such as pressing or clicking on a button, entering text, selecting an item from a menu, dragging-and-dropping an icon, and so on.

Let's imagine that a user of a word processor has the *goal* of writing and printing out a letter. This *goal* might be achieved with some combination of the following general tasks:

- Creating a new document

- Entering text

- Editing and proofreading text

- Spell-checking

- Adjusting page formatting

- Previewing

- Printing

To accomplish the task of creating a new document, the user might perform the following series of *actions* in the interface:

- Click on the "File" pull-down menu

- Click on the "New" menu option

- Enter a document title in a dialog box

- Click on the "OK" button to close the dialog box

It's important to understand that goals can often be achieved by means of various different sets of tasks, and tasks can often be achieved by means of various different sets of actions. So for the task of creating a new document, alternatively, the user might have used a shortcut keystroke such as Alt-N, or perhaps the user might have opened an existing document and re-saved it with a different filename.

And while there may be some cases where tasks can be achieved by following a strict step-by-step sequence of actions, in many cases, such as entering and editing text in a word processor, tasks are more of an ongoing or iterative process, and multiple tasks might become intermixed with each other as work is done towards reaching the goal.

The action cycle

An experienced user will usually know what tasks are needed to accomplish a goal, and can figure out what actions are needed to accomplish each task. New users learning how to use an application, on the other hand, are usually uncertain about what actions can be done to accomplish a task, and may even be uncertain about what tasks are necessary to achieve their goal.

Some users will seek out documentation or online help resources to find instructions on how to use the product. However, most users will begin by taking an exploratory approach.

When first trying to accomplish a task, a user will typically explore and inspect the interface for clues. Once the user has identified a potential action that may help move the user along the path to accomplishing the task and achieving the goal, the user will execute that action, and then observe what happens. If the results of the action — the feedback — matched what was expected, then the user will continue on with the next step in completing the task. If not, then the user may try an alternative action, or the decision might be made to modify the task or the goal.

A user will generally continue this cycle of searching for suitable actions, choosing actions, performing actions, and evaluating the results, until the goal has been satisfactorily achieved, or until the user gets stuck and needs assistance to continue.

Donald Norman elaborated on this process more formally in his book *The Design of Everyday Things* (Norman, 1990), describing it as the **seven-stage action cycle model**, which consists of the following steps:

1. Identifying an immediate goal

2. Forming an intention to act

3. Determining a plan of specific actions

4. Carrying out the actions

5. Observing the results by perceiving the state of the system and the world

6. Interpreting the results

7. Evaluating whether the actions had the desired results

These steps are repeated in an ongoing cycle — the evaluation of the effects of the actions informs the selection of the next goal — and so this model describes human-computer interaction as an continuous feedback loop between the user and the machine.

Mental models

As your users learn how to perform tasks with your application, they gradually form a *mental model* of how it works and how to operate it. A **mental model** is a conceptual representation in a user's mind of how a system works, and how to operate its interface. A user's mental model reflects the user's *current* understanding, and that understanding is subject to change as the user gains experience with the product, or forgets details over time.

When faced with a new situation, users rely on their mental models to reason about the situation and the system, and to make decisions and formulate strategies on how to proceed. Users will also form expectations for the application's behavior based on their mental models.

But mental models are not always *correct* representations of how a system works and behaves, and the mismatch between a user's incorrect mental model and the system's actual **implementation model** can explain many usability problems. It's important, therefore, for a system to be designed in such a way as to help users form a correct mental model of the system's operation.

What makes up a mental model?

Mental models are cognitive structures in peoples' minds. It's hard to say that mental models have any particular form or structure. A mental model is not inherently visual, although visual images do form an important part of a mental model.

A mental model for a software-based system consists of the following elements.

General appearance

A user will mentally form visual images of the "places" (screens, pages, tabs, windows, etc.) of the system that the user has encountered and is familiar with. But these mental images are typically very vague and imperfect; most users will not have photographic recall.

For a typical complex software application, users will become familiar with the general layout of the places they encounter frequently. The level of detail of mental images will vary depending on each user and the frequency of use.

For example, as a frequent user of Microsoft Word, I have a vague image of the layout of the main window in my mind, though without looking, I wouldn't be able to recall the exact sequence of icons in the toolbar or even what precise sequence of pull-down menus exists after *File* and *Edit*. I know some of the dialogs like *Font* and *Find/Replace* well enough that, even if the text of the labels and buttons were blurred, I could still recognize the dialogs by the "shapes" of their layouts. But my recall is not good enough to be able to sketch them out accurately.

Concepts, vocabulary, and rules

As we saw in previous chapters, every software-based system or product solves some sort of problem (though it may be a trivial problem, such as keeping the user entertained, in the case of a game).

The concepts, vocabulary, and rules involved in the context of that problem are referred to as the **problem domain**, the **business domain**, or the **application domain**.

For some systems, the problem domain is relatively small. The operator of an e-mail client only needs to understand a handful of concepts, like e-mail addresses and attachments. Other systems will demand much more in-depth knowledge and understanding of a domain. Imagine what a master operator in the control room of a nuclear power plant needs to know!

Some applications, like the nuclear power control system, must be designed with the assumption that the users already have the prerequisite knowledge of the domain, whether through education, training, experience, or some combination of these.

Other applications have the responsibility of communicating their unique concepts to the user. Games, being imaginary worlds rather than real-world problem-solving tools, are an extreme example of this. The first time you play, say, *Angry Birds*, you need to learn what objects are in the game and how they interact (in other words, the basic rules of the game).

Or, take Twitter as another example. To use Twitter, you need to understand what a "tweet" is, and you need to learn that you can follow other users and that other users can follow you. If you had never heard of and never used Twitter before, you'd most likely explore the Twitter website or app and figure out how it works via experimental self-discovery. In the somewhat unique case of something as popular as Twitter, the chances are that you might learn the concepts second-hand by watching a friend use it or by hearing about it in the media.

In many cases, users can grasp concepts without explicitly knowing the associated vocabulary and terminology. For example, web browser users can enter website addresses without knowing that the addresses are technically called URLs (*uniform resource locators*).

Additionally, users often don't need a full understanding of many concepts if the software handles the appropriate details for them. Users of a shipping postage calculator may only need of know *of* a customs duty fee; they do not need to know its precise rules and regulations, as they will trust the software to calculate the fee for them.

In many cases, users who aren't aware of all of the application's concepts, or don't understand them completely, are still often able to use the application effectively, if not optimally. Virtually all beginning users of Microsoft Word are unaware of the concept of styles, for instance, but they are still quite capable of producing documents.

Upcoming chapters on design principles will give us insights on how to structure applications to help users discover and learn key concepts.

Navigation map

Many applications consist of places (screens, pages, tabs, windows, etc.), which the user can "visit". When it is necessary for the user to differentiate between these places and to be able to get to them quickly, the user will gradually form a mental **navigation map** indicating how to get to the different destinations.

Navigation is often one of the actions needed to carry out a task in an application. For example, to purchase goods on an e-commerce site, you may need to navigate to the shopping cart page and then click on a *Checkout* button, which leads to a sequence of pages for finalizing the purchase.

Sometimes there may be more than one way to get to a location. For example, to get to the *Print* dialog box in most Windows applications, you can navigate to the *File* menu and choose *Print...*, or you can use the shortcut Ctrl-P, or you can click on the printer icon in the toolbar. The user may not be aware of all ways to navigate to a destination, and users aware of multiple options will tend to use only one of them frequently.

Action plans or strategies for accomplishing tasks or for reacting to situations or problems

Users may memorize *plans of actions* needed for carrying out certain tasks.

An **action plan** might take the form of a simple sequence of steps to follow. Or, with sufficient experience with the product, users may internalize a conceptual structure similar to a flowchart diagram that has various decision points and branches with steps to follow under different circumstances. (But note that most users will not actually have a literal visual depiction of a flowchart in their mind, and keep in mind again that the structure may not necessarily be complete or correct.)

Sometimes a user may not necessarily understand why a certain sequence of actions performs a particular task, but they've still memorized the sequence and are able to reproduce it. This can happen when the user has been taught how to perform a task in a training session, but some of the fundamental concepts (the "why" behind the actions) haven't been explained. It can also happen when the user has discovered by accident how to perform a task.

General heuristics and conventions

The user's mental model may include general **heuristics** — rule-of-thumb guidelines learned from experience — and conventions from a broader context that can be applied to the system at hand. For example, based on the user's experience with the operating system, one such heuristic might be, "to dismiss a dialog box, click on the *OK* button or click on the 'X' in the title bar".

Perceived implementation model

In some cases, a user may begin forming a general conception of how the product works internally, at some basic level, though this is never guaranteed.

For simple mechanical devices and machines, you are often able to see all of the moving parts, and you can mentally envision how the parts interact when the device is in operation. If you examine and manipulate a manual can opener, for instance, you can see how the edge of the can is pinched between the wheel and the blade, and you can imagine how turning the handle slices open the can.

For simple mechanical devices, seeing and understanding how the parts work can be helpful and may even be necessary for operating the device correctly. But for more complex mechanical devices, like the engine of an automobile, the inner workings are often too complicated for non-engineers to understand — and so such machinery is tucked out of sight. Automobile operators are offered simplified, abstract controls — like the gas pedal and the automatic gearshift — which eliminate the need to know how the engine works. In other words, the user's mental model of the underlying implementation can be extraordinarily simple (basically: "the engine consumes gas to run, so I need to make sure there's still enough gas in the tank"). The user's mental model can instead focus on the actions needed to make the car move: put the gearshift into *Drive* and depress the gas pedal.

For software products, designers need to hide the internal workings to the maximum extent possible. While some technically-sophisticated power users might try be able to reverse-engineer how the underlying algorithms and data storage schemes and communications protocols work, users should never have to know about such technical implementation details.

But even if users are perfectly shielded from unnecessary technical implementation details, they will still often be able to observe patterns in how the system operates and responds to inputs. From these observations and patterns, users will form simple implementation models, and implementation models on this level of abstraction are a good thing.

Let's say your application has an on-screen table containing a list of contacts, and there is an *Add* button to let the user add a contact to the list. The user observes that every time a new contact is added, it appears at the bottom of the list, below the other entries. Based on this observation, the user will tend to presume that the contacts are maintained in a sequential list, and new contacts are always simply added to the end of the list (rather than being added at the top of the list or being inserted at appropriate places in order to maintain alphabetical ordering or some other sort order).

This is a very simple and abstract form of implementation model, but it helps the user predict what will happen when the action of adding a new contact is performed, and when users encounter another similar-looking table, they will typically assume that the same behavior applies there as well.

Communicating an intended mental model to users

As a user interface designer, you'll have your own conceptual mental model in your mind of how the application will function. In order for users to be able to operate the application effectively, they will eventually have to have similar mental models in their minds.

One way of building up a mental model in a user's head is to provide a structured instructional curriculum that explains the product's concepts and operation. This may take the form of documentation or training. For most products, however, the vast majority of users will not read the documentation, and training, when available, is not always pedagogically effective.

Some users have the benefit of being able to watch other users use the application, and this can be a very effective way of learning the basic concepts and developing an understanding of how to perform tasks. Having an expert nearby whom the user can ask for assistance is also very helpful.

But without any training, documentation, or opportunities to watch and ask other users, the only way a user can figure out how to use the application is to simply start using it, and learn via trial-and-error.

The visual presentation of the application's user interface provides cues as to how to accomplish actions and tasks, and the behavior of the application provides feedback on whether the actions and tasks are having the intended effect. And so by continually exploring and experimenting with the application, the user will gradually build up a mental model of the application's functionality. With time and experience, it is hoped that the user's mental model will increasingly approximate the designer's conceptual model.

To use the terminology popularized by Donald Norman in *The Design of Everyday Things*, the conceptual model in the designer's mind is called the **design model**. The user's mental model is simply referred to as the **user's model**. And the visual presentation and the behavior that the product's user interface exhibits is what is called the **system image**.

And so to design a usable and learnable product, then, the designer's challenge can be viewed as *aligning the design model and the system image* in such a way that the system image accurately portrays the design model and enables users to develop their own users' models that approximate the design model as closely as possible.

As the completeness and correctness of a user's mental model increases, that user's skill at operating the application should very gradually approach that of the application's designer.

Structuring the system image to make an application learnable and understandable is tricky, and the remainder of this book concentrates on exploring how to do this by means of understanding psychological principles, design principles, design techniques, and usability testing and evaluation techniques.

Human memory

Learning to use a product involves learning and memorization, and operating a product often relies on the user keeping the context of the situation in short-term memory.

Human memory is complex and a little mysterious, and unlike electronic data storage, it is not perfectly reliable and predictable. In this section, we'll take a whirlwind tour of human memory, and then apply this knowledge to user interface design.

A model of memory

There are a number of psychological models of human memory. Most distinguish between short-term and long-term memory as separate but interrelated structures or systems in the brain. While there is no consensus on the "correct" model, one model useful for us is as follows:

- **Short-term memory** or **working memory** is a temporary store that can hold a small amount of information, such as a handful of words, numbers, or symbols, related to your current train of thought. Working memory decays very rapidly; the information can be lost when your attention is drawn to something else, and so you often have to rehearse or repeat the information to yourself to avoid having it disappear. The capacity of working memory is said to be about "seven, plus or minus two" items (Miller, 1956), and it's for this reason that North American phone numbers were chosen to be seven digits long — it's difficult to hold more than about seven digits in your mind when you hear a phone number and you're trying to write it down.

- **Middle-term memory** or **contextual memory** holds the information you need to be able to work on your current activity, but you won't permanently remember most of this information. For example, during a conversation, you'll have in mind the details of what has been discussed so far. Or if you're working on your tax return, you'll know where on your desk you've put your different papers and receipts and you'll remember some of the key numbers and details.

- **Long-term memory** is a more persistent store of knowledge and memories of experiences — facts, concepts, ideas, names, images, sounds, voices, places, emotional feeling states, and so on. Long-term memory also stores procedures and skills, for both cognitive and sensory-motor tasks. Long-term memory might alternatively be called **permanent memory**, but this is misleading as information is often subject to forgetting or "false recall".

How does memorization happen?

Memorization, the act of intentionally committing something from short-term memory to long-term memory, usually happens through repetition. Generally, the more often you encounter (see or hear) something, the more likely you are to remember it later. Studying involves actively and intentionally re-reading, rehearsing, and practicing.

But we also tend to remember information and experiences that are surprising, novel, important, or unusual without any repetition.

The exact nature of how the brain forms memories remains unknown, but it is likely that information and memories stored in long-term memory are somehow stored symbolically. That is, if you hear a professor telling you information in a lecture, you may memorize some of the information in the lecture, but you will probably not store a perfect audio recording of the professor's lecture. You may of course remember the professor's voice, especially if it is particularly unique, but this is separate from the information content of the lecture, which you can make use of in practical contexts without "playing back" the "audio recording" of the professor's voice.

There are some rare people who do have a perfect photographic memory, though, and most people can remember music precisely enough that they can distinguish if a later performance differs by only one note.

We tend to store information in logical groupings which psychologists call **chunks**. Memorization is most effective when a chunk is associated with other existing chunks of information in memory. **Associations** are logical connections or relationships between pieces of information. If you meet and get to know a new person, for instance, you'll associate the image of their face with their name and their other personal details you might learn, like their occupation and family members.

If you are trying to learn a complex concept or process, and you feel that your understanding is incomplete or insufficient because of unanswered questions, memorization and later recall will tend not to be as reliable as when you feel that you have a complete and logical understanding of the matter.

Recall and recognition

Recall of information from long-term memory is usually triggered by some **cue** or **prompt**. Seeing someone's face, for instance, can trigger you to recall that person's name.

Successful recall is never guaranteed. The more recently the information was memorized or accessed, though, the more likely you are to be able to recall it (the **recency effect**).

Successful recall of some piece of information is also more likely to occur when you've already recalled related information. It's as if related information is stored in adjacent locations in the brain, and by accessing information in a particular region, you "light up" that region, and then recalling other related information from that region becomes easier.

Sometimes you will struggle to recall something, and the information may or may not come to you at a later time. Sometimes recall is inaccurate; you recall incorrect information. You might misremember a formula when you're taking a math test, for instance. Sometimes you may have doubt about whether the recalled information is correct, but just as frequently, you may not recognize the error.

Often you may not be able to recall something, but you can **recognize** it when you see it. The information was in your memory, but for some reason it was "shrouded" and didn't lend itself to being accessed at that moment.

Forgetting

The less frequently a chunk of information or a skill is accessed from long-term memory, the more likely it is to be forgotten. This is natural — things that are relevant to your daily routines will be remembered, and additionally, they will be continually reinforced due to the recency effect. On the other hand, facts that you studied years ago but haven't needed, or the names of people whom you met years ago but haven't kept in contact with since, will tend to fade away.

But there are also many cases where letting information or skills languish for long periods of time won't necessarily guarantee that they will be forgotten. Highly-developed motor and cognitive skills that can be done unconsciously after much practice — like riding a bicycle or speaking a foreign language — can often still be performed with surprising levels of competence even after years of neglect.

Applying knowledge of human memory to user interface design

On the basis of this understanding of memory, memorization, recall, and forgetting, here are some guidelines to keep in mind when designing software:

- Structure your interface to reduce or eliminate the need to memorize and recall things. Donald Norman discusses the notion of "knowledge in the world" versus "knowledge in the head". For example, presenting a list of options in a menu is an example of "knowledge in the world": the user can view the menu, read and recognize the options, and make a selection without needing to memorize or recall anything. If you were to require the user to enter commands at a command-line interface, on the other hand, this would require the user to memorize and recall the commands, thereby requiring the user to store that knowledge "in the head", and making subsequent recall potentially subject to errors and forgetting.

- If a task has a defined sequence of steps, guide the user through the task flow step-by-step by presenting forms and controls in a logical, sequential order. If appropriate, consider offering a **wizard**-style interface, with multiple pages that can be traversed with *Previous* and *Next* buttons. Avoid forcing the user to remember a series of commands or how to navigate to various seemingly unrelated places to finish the task.

- While shortcut keystrokes and command-line interfaces are appreciated as time-savers by advanced users, you shouldn't make these the sole means of interaction, as they require memorization and recall. If you must rely on shortcuts or commands, make it easy to refer to a quick-reference chart or other help material.

- Make icons and names easily recognizable so that they can be found easily when scanning a list or menu. Icons can be clarifying if the images represent things that are concrete and recognizable. The icons also need to be easily differentiable from each other. If the user has to memorize and recall what an peculiar or abstract icon really means, or if the user must squint and try to puzzle out the difference between several nearly identical icons, then it defeats the purpose of using a graphical representation. An icon's image and a textual label should be shown together if the image is abstract or its meaning is unclear.

- If the user will have to work with ID numbers such as product or customer numbers, it can be advantageous to limit these to about seven or fewer digits or characters in length, if possible, so that it's easier to temporarily store the numbers in working memory.

- Arbitrary names are harder to remember and recall than names that accurately describe what they represent. When names don't match what they actually represent, not only do they become problematic to learn, but the additional memorization and recall add to the user's cognitive burden.

  Shell commands in Unix-based operating systems are particularly bad at violating this principle. For example, most Unix systems offer a command called "less" for showing the contents of a text file. The name "less" is a play on words; "less" is an enhanced version of another command called "more". ("more" is a filter command that lets you view a file or other stream of data in a page-by-page fashion; its name stems from the fact that it makes the console pause until you press the space bar to show "more" of the file or stream contents.) The name "less" doesn't in any way communicate what that command does; it's a banal pun by somebody trying to be clever. For the use case of showing the contents of a file, "list" would be one example of a more self-explanatory, more memorable, and equally concise name for this command.

- Offer a good online help system with search and index capabilities, or offer other forms of reference documentation, so that users can quickly look up instructions and information that they may have forgotten.

- In search and index systems, allow users to use synonyms and variations in case they can't recall the exact word or phrase (or the correct spelling) needed to identify something.

- Try to use commonly accepted, well-known, standard names for things rather than inventing your own terminology. Avoid using abbreviations or acronyms if they are not immediately obvious.

- Be consistent; don't make the user remember different ways of performing the same action in different contexts. I'm familiar with one enterprise system where some drop-down lists had to be opened with a Ctrl-L keystroke combination, while certain other drop-down lists had to be opened with Alt-F11. Technical limitations of the platform were given as the reason for that situation: fixed lists of values could be presented with the Ctrl-L drop-down list, where as dynamic lists of values required the alternative. However, I suspect a little more effort could have yielded a more user-friendly solution.

The impact of hardware devices on software ergonomics

A product that is **ergonomic** is designed in a way that helps reduce physical discomfort, stress, strain, fatigue, and potential injury during operation. While ergonomics is usually associated with physical products, the design of the a software application's interface also influences the way the user physically interacts with the hardware device on which the application runs. And ergonomics also extends to the cognitive realm, as we seek to design software that helps people work more productively, comfortably, and with a minimum of mental strain. We can do this by reducing the dependence on memorization, for example.

To create an ergonomically sound software application, it is important to first think about the properties and the context of use of the hardware device on which the application will run. For the majority of consumer and business applications, there are currently three main forms of general-purpose personal computing devices:

- **Desktop** and **laptop computers** with a screen, keyboard, and a pointing device such as a mouse or trackpad. These devices are comfortable for users sitting at a desk for a long period of time.

- **Tablet devices** with touchscreens. These devices have a form factor that is comfortable for sitting and consuming content (reading webpages, watching movies, etc.), but entering information and creating content via touch-screen control is generally not as comfortable and convenient as with a desktop machine.

- **Mobile phones** and similar devices such as portable music players. These devices are usually used for relatively short bursts of activity throughout the day and while on the go.

For more specialized applications, you might have a combination of software and custom-designed, special-purpose hardware. Examples include a vending machine that sells subway tickets, an automated teller machine, or an industrial thermostat control. If you are a designer for such a product, you may have responsibility for designing the form of the physical interface in addition to the software.

To give you an idea of some of the practical ergonomic aspects that you should keep in mind when designing for different devices, let's compare desktop computers with touchscreen tablets:

- Tablet devices with multi-touch touchscreens are pleasant and fun to use from an interaction standpoint because you can interact directly with on-screen elements by touching them with your finger. Desktop machines generally don't offer touchscreens (although at the time of publication, this is beginning to change). Touchscreens on desktop monitors can be uncomfortable for extended use, because reaching your arm out to the monitor places strain on the arm and shoulder muscles, and this quickly becomes physically tiring. Desktop setups thus rely on pointing devices such as mice and trackpads, which can be used with the hand and arm in a resting position on the desk. These pointing devices introduce a level of indirection, however: moving the pointing device moves a cursor on the screen.

- On desktop systems, there is a pointing device cursor (mouse arrow), whereas touchscreen devices have no such cursor. Some mouse gestures, such as hovering the cursor over a control, thus have no counterpart in touchscreen systems (and so, for example, pop-up "tooltip" messages that appear when you hover the mouse cursor over a control do not exist on touchscreen systems). On both desktop and touchscreen systems, however, a text cursor, called a **caret**, appears when a text field receives the focus.

- While a mouse may have multiple buttons, and clicks can be combined with holding down modifier keys (Control, Alt, Shift, Command, etc.), touchscreens don't offer as many activational options. When you drag your finger across the screen, is it to be interpreted as a scrolling gesture, or an attempt to drag and drop an object on the screen? Cut-and-paste and right-clicking to get a context menu are easy on a desktop machine, but on a tablet, such operations require double-touch or touch-and-hold gestures that are not always immediately evident.

- Fingers range in size substantially; young children have small, narrow fingertips, whereas some men have very thick, fat fingers. Touchscreen buttons and icons thus must be large enough to accommodate "blunt" presses without triggering other nearby controls. In contrast, the mouse arrow allows pixel-precise pointing, and so buttons and icons can be substantially smaller on desktop applications than on touchscreen devices.

- When the user is touching something on the screen, the user's finger and hand will obscure part of the screen, so you have to be careful about what you display and where, so that important information is not hidden. When pressing an on-screen button, the user's fingertip will obscure the button being pressed. Because button presses don't always "register", users seek visual feedback to see that the button press worked, and so you either need to make the buttons large enough so that the animation of the button being depressed is visible, or you should give some other clue when the user retracts the finger to show that the button was pressed (maybe pressing a *Next* button makes the application navigate to the next screen, which is very clear feedback that the button press was successful).

Auditory feedback, like a clicking sound, can also be useful as a cue that the button was pressed successfully. Some mobile and tablet devices can also vibrate slightly, to provide tactile feedback when a button is pressed.

- Mobile devices and tablet devices are often held by the user in one hand while standing, and so the user has only the other hand free to operate the touchscreen.

When designing a product, understanding the constraints and limitations, as well as the opportunities, of the hardware devices the software will run on will help you design appropriate and comfortable interactions.

Cognitive load and mental effort

Users interact with a software application by means of physical actions. These actions can include pressing keys and key combinations, typing for a sustained amount of time, precisely aiming a pointing device (homing the mouse pointer onto a target), and clicking the mouse or gesturing on the screen.

Performing each such action incurs a **cost** of time, physical effort, and some mental effort. In other words, performing an action requires the user to expend some energy.

In addition to the above physical actions, there are other actions that cost time, physical and mental effort, and energy, such as:

- Reading labels, titles, and instructions

- Choosing an option from a list or menu

- Scrolling

- Navigating

- Seeking (trying to locate something specific)

- Switching contexts (for example, switching between two windows, pages, or tabs)

- Switching visual attention (for example, reading text, then referring to an illustration, and then returning to the text)

- Recalling from memory a specific piece of information, such as a command name or an ID number

- Recalling from memory how to carry out a task sequence

- Waiting for a response from the system

- Recovering from some kind of distraction (like an unexpected pop-up dialog that is not directly relevant to the task at hand)

In general, users don't mind performing actions when the actions clearly help to make progress towards achieving a desirable goal, and when there seems to be some underlying rationale for why the actions are necessary.

However, being forced to undertake actions that are perceived as unnecessary quickly produces feelings of annoyance; the application is forcing the user to waste time and energy. With enough repeated annoyances, it is only natural that resentment will form towards the product (and its designers, who evidently have little respect for the user).

Therefore, we should obviously aim to design applications in such a way that any unnecessary actions, thinking, or waiting are eliminated.

But consider this situation: If we can take a design that requires ten mouse clicks to accomplish a task, and revise it so that it only requires seven mouse clicks, then we'd probably say that the revised design is superior, because three evidently superfluous mouse clicks were eliminated. But what if the first design didn't require much conscious thought; the user might have had to repetitively click *Next* ten times in a row in a wizard where all the default settings were acceptable. And perhaps the second design required a lot of thought as to how to set up various options in a very large, complex control panel. In this case, it sounds like the first design is the easier one to use, even though it involves a few more clicks.

So while we should generally aim to reduce the average number of physical and low-level actions a user must perform, we should really take a broader view. We must consider the *cognitive load* imposed by the task and the user interface.

Cognitive load refers how mentally taxing it is to do a task. It is essentially a way of referring to how much sustained attention and brainpower is required to do something.

The more complex a task is — that is, the larger the number of contextual details of the task that the user has to keep in working memory, and the more the task demands a high level of focused attention — the higher the cognitive load is for that task.

And so a good general design strategy is to reduce the user's cognitive load as much as possible. The title of Steve Krug's popular usability book, *Don't make me think!* (Krug, 2000), is a useful slogan to remember — reducing the amount of thinking the user has to do is arguably the single most important goal to consider when designing usable software products.

Thinking might just be the hardest kind of work there is. At least, it is the most avoided. For instance, most users of spreadsheets and word processors use a lot of repetitive manual keystrokes for, say, formatting content. While these users may suspect that there must be a more efficient way of doing the reformatting, they continue to use their trusted but labor-intensive methods, because thinking through the problem, investigating alternatives, and learning how to configure and use features like styles, macros, or scripting would involve more intense mental effort than just plowing through using manual techniques that require less thinking. While an alternative method would probably save time over the long run, most users doesn't want to spend the time and effort in the short term to figure out that alternative.

Types of thinking

Let's consider some of the different kinds of thinking that users of software might have to engage in. If your application requires some of the following kinds of thinking, it might be worth investigating whether you can restructure the design to reduce to some degree the need to engage in them:

- Determining what the next step in a procedure should be

- Holding things in working memory for the duration of the task

- Having to recall facts, commands, or procedures from long-term memory

- Having to memorize things in long-term memory

- Having to look up information from a reference source

- Making decisions or judgements

- Mentally integrating information from multiple sources

For many intellectual tasks, a lot of thinking goes on in the user's head, and the software only incidentally serves as a way to facilitate the activity and record the results of the thinking. For example:

- Creative output: coming up with ideas and generating the content of writing, audio, or visual art projects

- Problem-solving

- Reading and understanding long passages of text

- Actively conducting research with the goal of discovering, synthesizing, or creating new knowledge

For these higher-level activities, there's often little you can do to reduce the amount of thinking required, because the thinking involved has very little to do with the hands-on operation of the software. The best you can do is ensure that the software works reliably, generates good-quality output, and supports the task as best as possible.

So if your application provides access to academic journal articles, the search function should provide relevant results, which will reduce the amount of time the user spends searching, navigating, and reading. Likewise, if your application is a word processor and your user is writing a novel, there's little you can do to relieve the user of the very tricky mental work involved in creative writing, including developing a plotline, creating and fleshing out characters, and crafting the narrative and dialogue. But your application can aid the user in secondary ways, perhaps by offering support for organizing notes and materials, or by providing smarter tools and workflows for editing and proofreading.

Reducing the amount of all types of work and effort — both thinking and physical actions — will result in a product that is easier and more enjoyable to use.

Quantifying cognitive load and task efficiency

If we wanted to attempt to quantify the cognitive load — i.e., the thinking and effort involved — for performing a particular task, we could write out a list of the actions or operations that a user would have to do to carry out that task under normal circumstances. We could then estimate or assign a score, representing our idea of the effort involved, to each individual action, and then sum up all of the scores to get a total effort score for the task. We could then evaluate different design alternatives by comparing their scores.

The KLM-GOMS model, the *Keystroke-Level Model* for the *Goals, Operators, Methods, and Selection Rules* analysis approach (Card *et al.*, 1983), is one analysis technique based on this idea, but instead of assigning scores representing effort, an estimate of the time required to do each action is estimated instead. The amount of time it takes to complete a task is a good proxy for physical effort, although it does not accurately measure the intensity of mental effort.

Let's take a very condensed tour of the KLM-GOMS approach.

To accomplish a goal, the user will break the work into tasks, and for each task unit, the user will take a moment to construct a mental representation and choose a strategy or method for carrying out the task. This preparation time is called the **task acquisition time**, and can be very short — perhaps 1 to 3 seconds — for routine tasks, or much longer, perhaps even extending into several minutes, for creative design and composition tasks.

After the task acquisition, the user carries out the task by means of a sequence of actions or operations. The total time taken to carry out the actions is called the **task execution time**. Thus the total time required to complete a task is the sum of the task acquisition and task execution times.

To estimate the task execution time, KLM-GOMS defines basic operations (we assume here that we are dealing with a keyboard-and-mouse system):

Operation		Description	Suggested average values
K	Keystroking	Pressing a key or mouse button, including the Shift key and other modifier keys	Best typist: 0.08 s Good typist: 0.12 s Average typist: 0.20 s Worst typist: 1.20 s
P	Pointing	Moving the mouse pointer to a target on the screen	1.10 s
H	Homing	Moving a hand from the keyboard to the mouse or vice-versa	0.40 s
M	Mental operation	Mental preparation or thinking	1.35 s
R	System response operation	Time taken for the system to respond	varies

FIGURE 9-1

So to use the mouse to click on a button, we would have a sequence of operations encoded as "HPK": homing, to move the hand to the mouse; pointing, to move the mouse to target the mouse cursor over the button; and a keystroke, representing the pressing of the mouse button.

In addition to these operators, the KLM-GOMS model also includes a set of heuristic rules governing how the "M" operation, the mental operation, is to be inserted into an encoded sequence. For instance, "M" operations should be placed before any "K" and

"P" operations, except for various special cases. So the "HPK" sequence discussed above would become "HMPK". The suggested heuristic rules are quite complex and arcane, so please refer to the original article by Card *et al.* if you need to know all of the details. In actual practice, it will usually suffice if you simply insert "M" operations in places where you feel there is some thinking or decision-making effort involved.

As an example, let's consider the task of finding instances of a search term in a document in a text editor. One possible sequence of actions to accomplish this might be:

- Click on the "Search" menu

- Click on the "Find Text" item in the menu

- Enter "kittens" as the search term in dialog

- Click on the "OK" button

This can be encoded using KLM-GOMS and used to formulate an estimate of the average time required as follows:

Action/Operation	Encoding	Time (s)
Task acquisition	-	1.5
Click on the "Search" menu	H[mouse]	0.40
	MP["Search" menu]	1.35 + 1.10
	K["Search" menu]	0.20
Click on the "Find Text" item	MP["Find Text" item]	1.35 + 1.10
	K["Find Text" item]	0.20
	H[keyboard]	0.40
Enter "puppy" as the search term	7K[k i t t e n s]	7(0.20)
Click on the "OK" button	H[mouse]	0.40
	MP[OK button]	1.35 + 1.10
	K[OK button]	0.20
Total		12.05 s

FIGURE 9-2

Of course, we would expect a more skilled user to be able to accomplish the same task in substantially less time by using shortcut keystrokes rather than the mouse. You could do a separate analysis of each possible task sequence to compare the relative efficiency of each alternative.

There are obviously limitations to this kind of analysis; it provides a general rough estimate only, and it assumes that users know the right sequences of actions to complete a task. It also does not account for errors and mistakes. But when you are designing an interface and considering how to design an interaction, methods such as the KLM-GOMS model give you a way to compare the efficiency of different alternatives, and all other things being equal, the alternative that can be done in the least amount of time is the most convenient to the user, and often involves the least cognitive load.

Recreational and creative uses of software

Our discussion of cognitive load might make it sound like operating software is an arduous ordeal, and while this might be true for some enterprise systems, it's not the case for all software. Games require interaction with an interface, but this is not perceived as being work. Having to click 100 times to delete 100 spam comments on a blog would be considered intolerably poor design. Yet people will happily click hundreds of times when playing a game such as *Mah Jongg*. There are also games like flight simulators where players gain enjoyment from doing what others, such as aircraft pilots, do in their everyday jobs.

As well, when people get deeply involved in producing a creative work, whether writing a novel or drawing art, what might appear to be work to others may not be perceived as work by the artist. And so work that is voluntary and creative is simply more pleasurable than work that is involuntary and mundane. Motivating factors, like competition in games, can also change the way work is perceived.

Design techniques for reducing cognitive load

We've argued minimizing cognitive load is essential for making software more pleasant to use. Here are some tips and techniques to employ for reducing the cognitive load imposed by your software product:

- Use consistent naming, labelling, icons, and visual presentation to reduce any confusion.

- Avoid redundancy so that the same information doesn't need to be read and processed repeatedly.

- Put related things close together, and avoid forcing the user to switch between different tabs or windows or to scroll back and forth to find or enter information.

- Avoid distractions like pop-up dialogs that break the user's concentration and flow.

- Identify and eliminate any unnecessary steps. You might allow expert users to hide instructions and turn off warning messages.

- If your application has multiple tasks or screens that share similarities, be consistent in designing the visual appearance and workflow of these tasks and screens, so that once the user has learned how to use one, the same patterns can be applied to the others.

- Automate as much manual work as is reasonably possible. In some cases, though, you may want to allow experts to have the option of doing things manually if they need an extra level of control or precision.

- Where there is a list of steps to be followed, always make it clear how to do the next step. When possible, guide users through tasks with wizard-style interfaces rather than force users to memorize a complex procedure.

- Use visual cues and clues to avoid the need for memorization and recall. Allow options to be selected from menus instead of requiring users to memorize commands.

- Reduce delays and latency as much as possible. Give feedback quickly. If an operation will take a long time, use a progress bar or other indicator to show that the system is busy, and when possible, give an estimate of how much time the remainder of the processing will require.

- In productivity applications, opening the application with a blank document can be confusing for new users, as they may not know where to begin. When possible, offer to take the user to a tutorial in the online help system, or provide templates or sample documents so that users can modify an existing document and learn by following a pattern.

- Avoid forcing the user to memorize data in the short term. For example, in one enterprise system (the same one as mentioned previously, with the inconsistent drop-down lists), in order to accomplish virtually any use case, the user was required to visit a series of screens, and the same nine-digit customer number had to be re-entered in each window. This was absurd when the system could easily remember the context of which customer is being operated on and fill in this information automatically.

Flow states, focus, concentration, and productivity

Many kinds of software, including productivity applications and enterprise information systems, are intended to be used for sustained periods of time. Such applications should encourage the user to focus and work productively. Similarly, entertainment products

104

aim to immerse the user in an enjoyable experience.

Psychologist Mihaly Csikszentmihalyi described and popularized the concept of **flow**, which is the mental state of being completely focused on an activity. For a user who is in a flow state:

- Performance of the activity occurs naturally and unconsciously. Creativity and productivity are high.

- The user experiences deep concentration and immersion in the activity. The user is simultaneously alert and relatively relaxed.

- The user often becomes so engrossed in the activity that he or she is unaware of the passage of time (often described as "living in the moment").

- The difficulty of the activity is a good match for the user's skill; there is sufficient challenge to keep the user's interest, but not so much that the task seems impossible, and the activity is not so mundane that it causes boredom.

- The user is confident and has a sense of control over the situation.

- Usually, the user is working towards achieving a specific goal. (For some applications, the goal may not always be particularly productive; for games, the goal may be simply to finish one more level.)

Here are some things you should know about flow states with regard to software:

- Beginning users generally cannot be expected to be able to enter a flow state; it requires some level of comfort and competence with operating the application.

- It is often difficult to get into a flow state, and simply wishing to concentrate does not make it happen. Typically, it takes 15 minutes or more of struggling and working unproductively before one can "get into the groove".

- Interruptions such as phone calls and incoming e-mail notifications, and distractions such as chattering coworkers or a television in the same room, can pull a user out of a flow state. When returning to the activity after a distraction, it usually takes another period of time to get back into a flow state.

There is little you can do as a designer to *explicitly* help a user enter a flow state, but you can encourage and sustain concentration and flow by making the experience work smoothly and by minimizing or eliminating any repeated frustrations that might hinder the user from concentrating. Here are some design suggestions for doing that:

- Try to eliminate interruptions like modal pop-up dialogs that present notification and warning messages. Offer expert users the option of turning off any repetitive warnings.

- Keep the visual presentation simple. Brightly-colored images, and especially anything animated or blinking, can distract the user from reading text or concentrating on a work activity.

- When helping guide the user through task flows, make it obvious what the next step is, so that the user doesn't have to start exploring the interface, which easily leads to distraction.

- Avoid making the user switch repeatedly between different pages, screens, or tabs to find related information; each context switch can be disorienting and can cause users to forget what they were just doing.

- Make it easy for users to save any work in progress and then later pick up where they last left off.

- Show completion progress for lengthy tasks. When possible, reward the user for completing tasks; even a simple chime sound effect when some lengthy process is completed can be satisfying.

- Ensure that the system gives feedback promptly; especially in web-based systems, strive to reduce latency. Having to wait several seconds for confirmation that a button was pressed can become very annoying very quickly and can break the flow of work.

- It can be hard for humans to concentrate on multiple things at one, so when possible, don't make users manage multiple tasks at the same time. On the other hand, when the system is busy with a long-running process, you might give the user the option to have the process run in the background so that he or she can work on something else in the meantime. When users have to wait for an unknown length of time, they will frequently switch to something else while waiting (like checking e-mail or surfing the web).

If you are designing a typical software application, preventing distractions in the user's environment is out of your control. However, in some cases, you and your team may have the opportunity to influence the design of users' physical workspaces. For example, for an air traffic control operations center, in addition to designing the software itself, you may be able to influence the layout and design of the workstations and the office facility to prevent distractions.

Motivation, rewards, and gamification

Can software products be designed to motivate users and increase productivity?

If you're running an organization and your staff gets their work done using an enterprise application, you want to increase their productivity. Or, if you're running a community-driven website that relies on user-generated content, you want to encourage participation and repeat visits. Especially in a business setting, some of the tasks that have to be done are often tedious or unpleasant.

But there's one class of applications that tends to have little difficulty keeping users intensely focused and always coming back for more: Games. Some people think that some of the things that make gameplay addictive can also be applied to other kinds of applications. This is called **gamification**, and it's currently a hot fad.

What makes games addictive?

- First, there's the *voluntary* nature of game-playing. People are more likely to enjoy something when they're choosing to do it, rather than being required to do it.

- Second, games have *goals* and *rewards:* You want to get to the next level, and it's satisfying when you finally achieve it. Some games have elaborate systems of rankings, and as your skill improves, you get promoted; other games revolve around hunting for various desirable "items". And winning the game is ultimately the most satisfying reward.

- Third, as players achieve these goals and rewards, there is a sense of *progression* and an awareness that the player's *skill* is improving.

- Fourth, most online games are multiplayer games, and so there is an element of *competition*. Many people are driven to win and want to be the best. There is pride and social recognition in being at the top of the "high scores" leaderboard.

- Finally, multiplayer games can be a *social* experience, whether you're competing head-to-head with other players, or forming cooperative teams. For some people, games are a casual way to spend time and share social experiences with friends and family.

If these ideas make games fun and addictive, then can some of those ideas be brought to other products like enterprise applications and websites, and will this make those products more fun and addictive? It depends on the product and its users, but often the answer is yes — as long as it's not done in an overly gimmicky way.

Stack Overflow, a programming question-and-answer community website, is enormously popular. Much of that popularity today is due to the vast amount of content that often shows up at the top of the search results for programming-related queries. But how did they get all that content? It was created by the users, and a clever incentive system had a lot to do with it. Users accumulate points for successfully answering questions and earn "badges" as recognition of achieving certain milestones. Some badges unlock special privileges, like the ability to moderate discussions. And users with lots of points and badges enjoy respect and status for their contributions to the community.

Rewards systems can be effective for work that is easily measured. But you can breed resentment if the rewards system is not seen as reliable or fair. Creative work is particularly difficult to reward because objective metrics for measuring quality and even productivity are often impossible to define. For example, how would you create an algorithm to judge the quality of a graphic artist's logos? Or if one programmer took two hours and wrote 100 lines of code to solve a problem, and another took one hour but needed 200 lines, who is more productive?

One proxy for quality is popularity; on a community-driven website, you can let users "upvote" or give points to other contributors to reward them for good contributions. When the community is large and active, this system can be quite effective. This sort of peer voting is more problematic in a workplace setting, though. Asking employees in small teams to judge each others' work and hand out rewards rarely results in objective evaluations and can exacerbate office politics.

Reward systems are always well-intentioned, and yet they often lead to unexpected and unintended consequences. In a business environment, management will inevitably use these systems as a metric for judging and comparing workers' performance, even if that was not the original intention, and this can be problematic if the rewards system is not an accurate measurement of actual job performance. And metrics-based incentives encourage workers to game the system, to the detriment of the organization and its customers. I'm aware of a technical support call center that measured the time spent per call and disciplined workers whose average time per call exceeded a certain target. While the scheme was intended to reduce costs, it only had the effect of forcing workers to do anything possible to reduce call durations. So rather than try to actually resolve callers' issues, workers would unnecessarily forward calls to someone else or even give faulty but short answers so that they could hang up as soon as possible. This only led to an increased volume of calls from angry customers!

Competition can be a powerful motivator for some people; sales teams have used competition (such as salespeoples' results and rankings being posted in the hallway) as a motivator for years. But competition can be a turn-off for many others. If you structure the system so that there is only one winner, then you'll have one happy winner and the rest of your users will be unhappy losers. And on community websites, competition can discourage newcomers: How can a new user possibly compete against the obsessive-compulsive contributors who have been participating for years and have 50,000 points?

So if you're considering applying some of the ideas of gamification to your product, be sure that you understand your users, and be sure to think through all of the consequences.

Gamification can be very appealing to some audiences, and gimmicky to others. Established professionals, for instance, tend to be highly self-disciplined, take a lot of pride in their skills and accomplishments, and gain intrinsic satisfaction out of doing their job well. These people will be personally insulted by the notion that their work can be turned into a "game" with phony competition and incentives.

For professional users, the simple indication of progress on long tasks is probably the best reward. There is satisfaction in finishing a task, and for longer tasks, it's reassuring to know that you're making progress towards completion. So in a data-entry-centric application such as income tax software, it can make sense to break down data-entry forms into sections or pages that be checked off when complete. A graphical progress meter showing the percentage of work completed and work remaining can also be very useful. Figure 9-3 shows an example of a progress indicator on LinkedIn's profile editing page:

FIGURE 9-3

Because there is satisfaction derived from completing tasks, it is a good idea to break lengthy work sessions into smaller task units whenever possible. For example, reading a 500-page book with 50 small chapters tends to be more satisfying than reading a 500-page book with only 5 big chapters, because there's a feeling of completion and accomplishment when you reach the end of a chapter.

10

Design principles for usability

In this chapter, we'll explore some of the basic principles and concepts that are critical for understanding why some designs are more usable and learnable than others. We'll also look at concrete ways of applying these ideas to the design of software and user interfaces.

Norman's design principles for usability

Donald Norman, in his influential book *The Design of Everyday Things* (Norman, 1988), introduced a set of basic design principles and concepts that are now considered foundational in the study of usability: *consistency, visibility, affordance, mapping, feedback,* and *constraints*.

Consistency

One of the major ways that people learn is by discovering **patterns**. New situations then become more manageable and navigable when existing pattern knowledge can be applied to understanding how things work. **Consistency** is the key to helping users recognize and apply patterns.

In general, things that look similar should do similar things. For example, if we learn that protruding surfaces with labels on them are buttons that can be pressed, then the next time we see a new protruding surface with a label on it, we'll tend to recognize it as a pressable button.

Likewise, behavior and conventions should exhibit consistency across similar tasks and actions. For example, the *QuickBooks* accounting package makes a chime sound as audible feedback whenever a record is successfully finalized and saved, and this is consistent, no matter whether you're editing a invoice, a cheque, or a quote.

Inconsistency can cause confusion, because things don't look or work the way the user expects them to. Forcing users to memorize exceptions to the rules increases the cognitive burden and causes resentment. Attention to consistency is important for instilling confidence in the product; it gives the impression that there is a logical, rational, trustworthy designer behind the scenes.

Your application should be consistent internally, but should also strive to be consistent with external things in the environment in which it used. In particular, for desktop and mobile applications, you should aim to understand and conform to the user interface guidelines for your operating system or platform. Consistency with these standard conventions helps reduce the number of new things a user needs to learn.

Visibility

Users discover what functions can be performed by visually inspecting the interface and seeing what controls (menus and menu items, icons, buttons, etc.)are available. For tasks that involve a series of steps, having clearly-marked controls in a visible location can help the user figure out what to do next.

According to the principle of **visibility**, usability and learnability are improved when the user can easily see what commands and options are available. Controls should be made clearly visible, rather than hidden, and should be positioned where users would expect them to be. Placing controls in unexpected, out-of-the-way locations is tantamount to hiding them and making them invisible.

Functionality which does not have a visual representation can be hard to discover and find. For example, keyboard shortcuts save time for expert users, but when a keyboard shortcut is the only way to activate a command, then a new user will have no way of discovering it, except by accident, or by reading the reference documentation. If a command is presented in a pull-down menu with the shortcut listed next to it, though, then the command gains some visibility, at least when the menu is opened.

The principle of visibility should not necessarily be interpreted to mean that every possible function should have a prominent button or icon on the screen — for any complex application, there would be so many buttons and icons that the screen would become crowded and cluttered, and it would be difficult to find the right button. As discussed above, pull-down menus are an example of a compromise: the commands are visible when the menus are opened, but remain tucked out of sight most of the time. And in a full-featured application, you may want to consider only presenting the commands and controls that are relevant to the user's present context. In Photoshop, for example, one of the toolbar areas shows the options for the current drawing tool and omits any settings that are irrelevant for that tool. And in Eclipse, **perspectives** can be used to show only the panels and toolbars that are relevant for specific task activities.

Affordance

An **affordance** is a visual attribute or physical property of an object or a control that gives the user clues as to how the object or control can be used or operated.

Alternatively stated, we might say affordances are the manipulable parts of the system that allow us to interact with the system.

Door handles are the typical example used for explaining affordances:

- A round doorknob on a door invites you to turn the knob to open the door. We say that the doorknob *affords* (or allows) turning.

- A flat plate invites you to push on the plate to push the door outwards. It affords pushing.

- A graspable handle invites you to pull on the handle to pull the door open towards you. It affords pulling, but might also afford pushing.

The shapes and appearance of a door's handle thus present clues as to how the door can be manipulated. But the presented visual clues must accurately match how the affordance can really be operated; if a door handle *appears* to be pullable, but in actual fact you the door can only be opened by pushing it outwards, then the affordance is potentially misleading, and users could be frustrated when their initial attempts to open the door fail.

Applying the concept of affordance to graphical user interfaces, you can use visual cues to make controls look clickable or touchable. One common technique is to give on-screen controls the illusion of being three-dimensional and raised off the screen by means of the careful use of colors to simulate lighting and shadows. Dials and sliders can be made to look like real-world physical controls, and their shapes give clues as to how to manipulate them.

Whenever possible, you should use the standard controls (or "widgets") provided by the operating system or platform. This makes the controls easily recognizable because they are familiar to the user from experience with other applications on that platform.

Design conventions are another means of providing affordance cues. For example, underlined blue text is a standard convention for representing a textual hyperlink on a webpage. There is nothing inherently obvious about underlined blue text that makes it mean "I'm a clickable link", but it has become a widely-used standard convention that users have learned.

In desktop systems with pointing devices, another way of showing affordance is to change the shape of the mouse pointer when the mouse pointer is moved over a control. The mouse pointer may change from an arrow to a hand to indicate that a button is pressable, for instance. **Tooltips**, or small pop-up messages that appear when the mouse pointer hovers over a control, can provide additional assistance.

One particularly challenging thing to show affordances for is indicating that some element can be dragged-and-dropped, or that some element has a context menu available by right-clicking on it. There are no standard conventions for indicating these, and it is difficult to imagine an effective way of indicating these possibilities without introducing excessive visual clutter.

Mapping

Pressing a button or activating a control generally triggers the system to perform some function. There is a relationship, or **mapping**, between a control and its behavioral effect. You should always aim to make these mappings as clear, explicit, and straightforward as possible. You can do this by using descriptive labels or icons on buttons and menu items, and by using controls consistently.

Controls should also be positioned in logical ways, perhaps mimicking a real-world object, or adhering to general conventions. For instance, it's obvious that a slider control to adjust the left-right balance of stereo speakers should increase the volume of the left speaker when the slider is moved to the left. Or if you have an ordered list or a sequence of steps, these should naturally be positioned in top-to-bottom and/or left-to-right order (at least in the context of languages that are read in a left-to-right and top-to-bottom order).

The flight stick in an aircraft or flight simulator might be considered by some to have a non-conventional mapping. Pulling the stick towards you (usually perceived as a downward motion) causes the aircraft's nose to point upward, while pushing the stick away from you (perceived as upwards) causes the aircraft's nose to point downward. This is because the position of the flight stick controls the flaps on the wings, and if the flaps are down, the aircraft will climb. The mapping becomes natural for a trained pilot, but it might initially seem backward to new flight simulator users, who have to learn that pressing the "down" arrow key makes the aircraft go "up".

Feedback

If you press a button and nothing seems to happen, you're left wondering whether the button press actually registered and was recognized by the system. Should you try again? Or was there a delay between the button press and the expected action?

The principle of **feedback** states that you should give users a confirmation or an acknowledgement that an action has been performed successfully (or unsuccessfully). We might distinguish between two types of feedback:

- **Activational feedback** is evidence that the control was activated successfully: a button was pressed, a menu option was selected, or a slider was moved to a new position. This evidence might be provided with visual feedback; an on-screen button can be animated to give the appearance of being depressed and released. Physical controls can provide tactile feedback; you can feel a button moving and clicking as you press and release it. Auditory feedback could also be provided in the form of a sound effect.

- **Behavioral feedback** is evidence that the activation or adjustment of the control has now had some effect in the system; some action has been performed with some result. For example, in an e-mail client, after clicking the *Send* button, the dialog with the e-mail text may close, or you might get a confirmation message in a pop-up dialog. Additionally, the e-mail will be listed under the *Sent* folder.

One business system I've encountered offered a menu option for generating a report. When this menu option was selected, nothing appeared to happen. Because no feedback was provided, it was unclear whether the report generation was triggered correctly, and if it was, it was unclear whether the report was generated successfully. It turned out that a report file was created in a certain location in the file system, but the system did not tell the user where to find this file. Nor, in the case of an error, was the user informed of the situation. This system could have been improved by giving the user proper feedback; at the minimum, a confirmation should have been provided indicating that the report was created successfully and how to access it. Better yet, the report should have been automatically opened for viewing as soon as it became available.

Constraints

Interfaces must be designed with rules and restrictions in mind so that the system can never enter into an invalid state. **Constraints,** or restrictions, prevent invalid data from being entered and prevent invalid actions from being performed.

Constraints can take many forms. Here are some examples:

- A diagramming tool for drawing hierarchical organizational charts will prevent the boxes and lines from being dragged-and-dropped and rearranged into configurations that are not semantically legal (i.e., not a valid hierarchy).

- Word processors disable the *Copy* and *Cut* commands (indicated by greying out the commands in the pull-down menu) when no document content is currently selected.

- The dots-per-inch setting on a document scanning application is often controlled by a slider that restricts the chosen value to be within a range such as 100 to 400 dpi. This is a good example of a control that presents a constraint visually.

- The physical shapes and configurations of hardware devices affect how they can be used. For example, a USB cable's plug can only fit into the socket in one orientation; the design prevents the plug from being inserted upside-down.

Norman's principles of *consistency, visibility, affordance, mapping, feedback*, and *constraints* are important for the design and evaluation of user interfaces. The proper application of these principles helps give users the clues they need to discover the behavior of your product, and encourages the formation of accurate mental models of how the application works.

An additional usability principle worth exploring is *good naming*.

The importance of good naming

Humans use language to think and communicate, and when we think and speak about things and concepts in the world, we use **names** or **labels** to identify those things. It's usually pretty difficult to talk about something if it doesn't have a name! Names are *linguistic handles* that we can use to refer to both concrete and abstract things in our speech and writing.

Naming things in your application is a key part of design that is all too often overlooked.

Things in your application need to be named and labelled so that users can know where they are, what data they're looking at, and what actions they can perform. Good names and labels help the user form a correct mental model, and so it is important to speak the user's language, using vocabulary and concepts that are familiar to the user.

Precise and consistent naming is also important so that unambiguous instructions can be formulated, such as, "In the *Search* dialog, under the *Advanced* tab, uncheck the *Case sensitive* checkbox."

What kinds of things are typically given names in software applications?

- "Places" such as pages, screens, dialogs, and tabs

- Menus and menu items

- Tasks (the names of tasks may not necessarily be exposed to the user in many applications, however)

- Controls such as buttons, icons, checkboxes

- Descriptions of data elements (e.g., field names and column headings)

- Objects, classes, tables, records, files, and other forms of persistent data collections almost always need to be uniquely identified (though not all of these may be exposed to the user), and unique identifiers such as customer IDs or social security numbers could be considered to be names

- Domain-related or interface-specific concepts, constructs, and abstractions, such as "contribution limit" in a pension administration system, or "layer" in Photoshop

Names are used for **identification** of things, as well as **differentiation** between things. If two things are given the same name, then that name is ambiguous, because it could refer to either of the two things. Imagine you work in an office where there are two people named John: John Smith and John Thompson. If your boss asks you to "please pass this letter on to John," then without additional information, you can't be sure which John your boss is referring to.

In other words, "John" is not a unique name within the **context** of your office. It is ambiguous because it could refer to either John Smith or John Thompson. To eliminate the ambiguity, you have to add enough *qualifying* information to uniquely identify the target. So "John Smith" would be ideal, although "John S." or "John in Accounting" might also suffice.

So ideally, names will be **unique** within the context in which they are used. You may know a Suzanne in your office and a Suzanne at your yoga studio. If someone from the office mentions Suzanne's name, you'll probably assume they're talking about the Suzanne in the office, whereas if someone you know from the yoga studio mentions Suzanne, you'll probably assume they're talking about Suzanne from the yoga studio. Because of the two different contexts, you're usually able to make a reasonable assumption about who is being referred to.

In the world of software, naming contexts are usually referred to formally as **namespaces**. If you were to make a list of all the names within a namespace, it is ideal if all the names are unique, because they can then all be differentiated from each other.

Here are some additional guidelines and things to keep in mind when you are choosing names for concepts, objects, places, commands, and other things in your application:

- Does the name accurately describe or summarize its target? For instance, a tab named *Address* is accurately named if the tab contains a customer's address information. But if the tab is then redesigned so that the customer's phone number and e-mail address are also displayed, then *Address* would no longer completely and accurately describe the contents of the tab, because the tab shows additional, non-address information that a user would not reasonably expect to see there. Perhaps *Contact Details* might be a more accurate title in this case.

  While this is an obvious guideline, it is also often overlooked as changes take place incrementally over time.

- Is the name free of ambiguity? If not, consider a different name or add adjectives to make the name more specific. For example, if you label a field *Profit*, will it be clear from the context whether this refers to the gross or net profit?

- Consider whether the level of abstraction is suitable for your audience and context. For example, the name *Universal Serial Bus* is an technically accurate name from a hardware design perspective, but average consumers don't know and don't care what *serial* and *bus* mean; the details of computer architecture is irrelevant to consumers. *FireWire* is a cleverer name for marketing purposes, because the name does not expose unnecessary technical details, it hints at the benefits (speed), and the rhyming and repetition in the name makes it more memorable.

- Names should be of a reasonable length, as excessively long names are hard to remember and time-consuming to read and write. On the other hand, don't try to shorten a name to the point where it no longer clearly and uniquely identifies the target. Yes, abbreviating *John Smith* to *JS* makes the name shorter, and may be suitable in a particular context, but *JS* will be ambiguous if there is also a Jane Smith or James Schmidt in the same context. Abbreviations and acronyms increase the chances of misinterpretation and so should be used with restraint, except for well-known or domain-specific cases that you're certain your user audience will understand. For example, *VAT* for *Value-Added Tax* is a well-known acronym in the UK, but is unfamiliar (and usually irrelevant) to most users in the US.

- Whenever possible, use existing standard terminology. If there are multiple synonymous terms for the same thing, like *Income Statement* and *Profit & Loss Statement*, choose one as the standard and use it consistently and exclusively in your application.

- The first letter and first syllable, or the first word in a compound word, are the most strongly memorable and differentiable. Suffixes are the least differentiating and memorable.

The sprawling city of Calgary, Alberta, Canada requires all streets within each demarcated suburban community to have names that begin with the same three letters. As shown in Figure 10-1, the Taradale suburb, for instance, is a maze of streets with names like Taradale Drive, Taradale Close, Tarrington Close, Tararidge Close, Tararidge Crescent, Taracove Road, Taracove Landing, Taracove Crescent, Taralea Park, Taralea Green, Taralea Way, Tarawood Grove, and Tarawood Lane. This can make finding a particular address while driving rather difficult. "Tararidge Crescent" would be a very unique name in a community with street names like Bay Street, 5th Avenue, and so on, but since all the names in this community sound nearly identical, a high cognitive load is imposed by the task of trying to remember an address and simultaneously comparing it against virtually identical alternatives.

Calgary's Taradale suburb (courtesy of Google Maps; map data copyright 2012 Google)

FIGURE 10-1

- Within each naming context, names should be consistent in terms of phrasing and capitalization. In a menu, for instance, having both *Add New Customer* and *Customer Editor* in the same list would be awkward, as the phrasings are not parallel. The former starts with a verb and describes an action, while the other is a noun phrase that describes a place in the application. Using the pair *Add New Customer* and *Edit Customer* would be more consistent.

  Likewise, *Add new customer* and *Edit Customer* are inconsistently capitalized, and while most people will not notice this sort of thing, your more literate and attentive users will notice. This kind of sloppiness won't inspire confidence amongst that group.

- Although we don't usually consider numbers to be names, numbering systems like social security numbers, passport numbers, and phone numbers are essentially a form of naming, as they are intended to serve as handles for uniquely identifying items and differentiating them from other similar items within a particular context.

- For product names, distinctiveness and descriptiveness are important. When selling internationally, try to ensure that your product's name is free of negative connotations in all of your markets. For example, *Siri*, the iPhone feature, sounds like the Japanese word for "buttocks", and a *Mist* air freshener probably wouldn't sell very well in Germany, because that is the German word for "manure".

- Names, and especially product names, should be easily pronounceable. When presented with the name in written form, people should not have to ask, "How do you say that?" And when someone hears the name being spoken, it should be easily recognizable, and the listener should, ideally, be able to spell it without hesitation. (YouTube is a great product name, but if you had never heard of it and someone mentioned the name to you, would you interpret it as "YouTube" or "UTube"?) Intentional spelling and punctuation variations like "Flickr" and "del.icio.us" can be distinctive, but have the trade-off that people will be forever misspelling them. Also, be consistent with your branding; is the correct spelling Walmart, Wal-Mart, or WAL*MART? That retailer has itself used all three variations at different times and in different contexts.

11

Creating a positive user experience

In the next chapters of this book, we will explore the design process. But before we plunge into the details of conceptualizing and designing a software application, let's take a brief moment to revisit our goal of creating a positive user experience. As designers, we'd like to know the characteristics of products that exhibit a positive user experience, so we can work to incorporate those in our design. We'd also like to know what things cause a negative user experience, so we can work to avoid those things.

In general, a product with a positive user experience will tend to have many of the following characteristics:

- It lets the user feel that he or she is in control.

- It lets the user develop a feeling of confidence and competence.

- It enables high productivity and efficiency, and enables and encourages the user to enter a flow state with sustained focus and concentration.

- It allows simple, routine tasks to be completed without much conscious and deliberate thought.

- It produces good quality output.

- It is aesthetically appealing.

- It exhibits acceptable performance.

- It produces correct and trustworthy results (for example, calculations give the correct results).

- It makes it easy to correct errors and mistakes.

- It is stable and reliable.

- It inspires trust and confidence by giving the impression that there is a logical, rational, intentional design behind it.

- It gives the user a generally pleasant feeling of satisfaction during use (and in the case of a game, it may even be considered addictive).

Note that not all of these characteristics may apply to all types of products, and since these characteristics are subjective and not easily measurable, they don't lead themselves to easy checklist-style verification.

A positive user experience is also characterized by the absence of any serious problems and annoyances.

If we re-examine our list of positive characteristics and simply observe the converse of each one, we see that a negative user experience can be had by a user of a product that has one or more of the following characteristics:

- It leaves the user feeling that he or she is not in control.

- It makes the user feel dumb, incompetent, or inadequate.

- It hinders the user from achieving productivity and efficiency, and doesn't let the user enter a flow state.

- It requires a lot of thinking to figure out how to do relatively simple or routine tasks.

- It produces output that is flawed or substandard (for example, fonts are rendered with a jagged appearance, or reports are produced with sloppy formatting, or software code is generated that doesn't compile).

- It looks disorganized, cluttered, or otherwise aesthetically unappealing.

- It is slow, with delays and lagginess that are frustrating and hinder the flow of work.

- It may produce unreliable results.

- It makes it difficult or tedious to find and correct errors and mistakes.

- It is unstable, unpredictable, and buggy, impairing the user's trust (for instance, the user may worry about losing work or having data corrupted).

- It gives the overall impression of a muddled, confused design.

- It causes the user feelings of annoyance and frustration, rather than satisfaction.

Here are some additional issues that can negatively impact the user experience:

- *Excessive complexity:* Excessive complexity makes a product hard to learn, and makes it more likely for users to make mistakes. These difficulties can cause the user to feel overwhelmed, incompetent, and embarrassed.

  Products that offer substantial functionality will, by nature, tend to have complex interfaces, and realistically, it is seldom possible to eliminate all of the complexity. But most applications will have relatively simple tasks that are carried out frequently, and for these tasks, it should be possible to carry them out with a minimum of steps. The advanced commands and options that expert users require could be tucked out of the way in additional menus, tabs, or slide-out panels.

- *Too much work:* Users resent products that make them carry out repetitive, mundane tasks that could have been automated. It is also frustrating when unnecessarily tedious effort is required to produce good quality output. For example, one diagramming tool I've used allowed elements to be moved by two or more pixels, but not by one pixel, making it a unnecessarily painstaking process to create diagrams with aligned elements.

- *A conceptual design that conflicts with the user's past knowledge and experience:* If the product's view of the world or the domain, including things like terminology, concepts, and processes, doesn't match what users already understand, then users will have a hard time learning and conforming to the product's alien way of thinking.

Usability issues caused by violations of design principles

Many usability problems can be interpreted as the result of violations of design principles. Let's revisit Donald Norman's design principles to see how such violations might impair the user experience:

- *Lack of consistency:* An interface that exhibits inconsistencies in visual layout, labelling, or behavior makes it harder for users to detect and learn patterns and relationships, which makes it harder to form mental models. Inconsistencies force users to memorize and remember exceptions to rules, increasing the cognitive load.

- *Poor visibility of controls and information:* If users can't locate the specific controls or information they are looking for, frustration will result. Significant time can also be wasted when users are searching for the means of carrying out desired actions, but cannot determine what the appropriate controls or gestures are.

- *Poor affordance cues for controls:* When controls don't give appropriate visual clues as to how they can be operated, some controls may not even be perceived as controls. Functionality is effectively hidden if the user cannot discover the means of activating it. A common example is the case where a user does not realize that a context menu can be opened by right-clicking on an icon or other object.

- *Poor mapping cues for controls:* When controls don't clearly indicate what actions they perform, confusion can result if the behavior does not match the user's expectations.

- *Insufficient feedback:* Without timely and clear feedback, the user can be left wondering whether a control was properly activated and whether the intended action was successfully performed.

- *Lack of constraints:* Without appropriate rules, validations, limits, and other constraints, users may be able to perform invalid operations, use controls in invalid ways, or enter invalid data. These problems can create unexpected results, create errors, or cause the system to enter an unstable and unpredictable state.

Can a product succeed despite a poor interface?

A product with a poor interface can still succeed commercially, and users can report overall satisfaction with it, if the product provides great value. Examples of value include enjoyable emotional experiences such as social interaction, or quantifiable business benefits, such as making money, saving money, or reducing the risk of some negative event. In such cases, users can tolerate the poor user interface because the value that the product provides outweigh the negative impact of the poor user interface: the overall user experience is still positive.

While it may be possible for some products to succeed despite usability issues, you can increase the chances of your product becoming a commercial success by giving it a great user interface and a great user experience. In the following chapters, we'll begin learning the design techniques needed for doing just that.

12

Designing your application's interaction concept

Let's now turn to the process of designing your product. To begin, we will first take a look at planning and designing the *interaction concept* for your application.

An application's **interaction concept** is a basic summary description of the designer's fundamental idea of how the application's user interface will work. An interaction concept describes how the interface is presented to the user and the general means by which users interact with the interface to complete their tasks.

Because usability problems tend to emerge when key issues like navigation, workflow, and transactions haven't been thought all the way through, it is worthwhile spending time on thinking about these issues and explicitly designing and evaluating solutions. However, not everything can or should be decided at the very beginning of a project. Preliminary initial decisions (and even guesses) will often have to be made, and these can then be revised and refined as the project goes on.

However, some fundamental things can be difficult and costly to change once product development is in full swing, and so these things — what we might call the **architectural design** — should receive special attention early on in the project.

It is possible to describe an application's interaction concept by writing a formal specification document, and for large teams building large products, this can be a reasonable approach. But as we've discussed in previous chapters, a formal document is not the only way to document and communicate design decisions. Writing a specification document can help force the team to think through and decide on key issues, but a formal interaction concept document can also be difficult to write because many things, like the visual design, are very difficult to specify completely and accurately in writing.

A more agile approach that can be successful is the combination of prototyping and minimal, lightweight documentation. Prototyping can be a very effective way of trying out different design ideas, getting feedback through peer reviews and usability testing, and then representing and communicating the intended design. A prototype alone cannot capture and communicate all of the design decisions and rationale, though, so lightweight written records can be used to supplement it.

In this chapter, we'll explore the following items and issues that you should consider when designing an application's interaction concept:

- a choice of one or more fundamental interaction styles;
- the basics of the information architecture, which may include:
  - a data model,
  - a naming scheme, or a glossary of preferred names and labels,
  - a navigation and wayfinding scheme, and
  - a search and indexing scheme;
- a framework for interactions and workflow;
- a transaction and persistence concept; and
- the general visual design framework for the product-wide look-and-feel.

Not all of these items will be applicable to all types of products and applications.

Defining your application's interaction style

One of the first things to be decided in creating your application's interaction concept is to decide on the general interaction style, by which we mean the fundamental way that the application presents itself to the user and allows functionality to be used.

To give you ideas for structuring your application, the following list gives some examples of major interaction styles. There is much overlap between some of these classifications, and many applications employ a combination of these styles. A video editing application, for example, combines aspects of the direct manipulation and control panel styles.

- **Form-filling**: The interaction revolves around the user entering data into on-screen forms.

- **Menu-driven**: The user controls the system by choosing options or commands from menus.

- **Command-line**: The user controls the system by entering commands or queries. There may be the ability to create scripts or programs containing multiple commands.

- **Conversational**: The interaction focuses around a give-and-take dialogue between the system and the user. Generally, one side asks the other questions. Depending on the system, the user may engage in the conversation using natural language (textual or vocal), a specialized query language (which then overlaps with the command-line style), or by picking options from a menu (this overlaps with the menu-driven style). For example, medical expert systems ask a series of questions about a patient's symptoms in order to narrow down the problem and suggest a diagnosis.

- **Direct manipulation**: The user operates the application by creating, moving, or otherwise manipulating objects on the screen. For example, in Photoshop, the user draws images or edits photos by directly drawing on and manipulating the canvas. A word processor lets the user write and manipulate text on a visual representation of a page. An automobile racing game lets the user steer the car.

- **Control panel**: The display simulates gauges, buttons, and other controls normally found on a traditionally hardware-based device or control panel, such as an industrial process control board, a stereo, a dashboard, or aircraft flight controls.

- **Content consumption**: The application serves mainly to present audio, video, or textual content to the user for consumption. Most of the user's actions revolve around navigating the content. Video players and book readers are examples.

For many applications, the choice of interaction style or styles is self-evident, but thinking through alternative or unconventional styles of presenting functionality can sometimes lead to ideas that differentiate your product from others in the market.

Designing the information architecture

Information architecture is concerned with organizing information — concepts, entities, relationships, functionality, events, content — into a coherent structure or "information space" that is comprehensible, navigable, and searchable.

Designing the information architecture for a software application or website involves thinking about the following:

Data model

In Chapter 7, we examined the importance of understanding the terminology, concepts, and objects in your application's domain. Identifying and recording the entities, the attributes and operations of each entity and the relationships between the entities produces a data model. The data model can be argued to be a part of the application's interaction concept, as it helps define what the product is about, and because the entities, attributes, and operations will have an impact on the visual design and interaction behavior.

Naming scheme and glossary

As we learned in Chapter 10, a coherent and consistent system of naming and labelling is important for helping users form a correct mental model of how the application works. Deciding on the official names for key elements and processes in your application is a good idea, and this can be recorded in the interaction concept.

For applications that deal with very complex, specialized domains, it will often make sense to create a glossary which defines the official, preferred terminology for the entire application. In that case, the interaction concept can link to or refer to the glossary.

Designing navigation and wayfinding

This book has been using the term "places" as a general term to refer to locations or containers that can present content and controls. Places might be pages in a web application, screens in a mobile or tablet application, or windows and dialogs in a desktop application. "Places" could also refer to subdivisions such as panels, tabs, and subsections within a page, screen, window, or dialog.

If your product has many such places, your design must help users determine:

- where they currently are,

- where they can go, and

- how to get to where they want to go.

Designing navigation and wayfinding involves thinking about the following aspects:

Identification of places using names or titles

Generally, each place should be clearly labelled with a title, so that users can determine what place they are currently looking at, and so that they can differentiate that place from other places. Assigning each place a title also allows the places to be referred to in menus, instructions, and help text.

Examples of place titles include a *Find and Replace* dialog box, a *Departures* page on an airport website, the *Settings* screen in a mobile phone application, or *Level 5* in a video game. In some applications, places can take on user-assigned names. For example, in a document-oriented application like a word processor, the title of a window or tab will be the filename of the document being displayed there.

Presentation of places

Depending on the type of application, you may need to decide on questions such as the following:

- Can the user view only one place at once? Or can the user have multiple places open at once, such as multiple documents in a word processor, multiple sheets in a spreadsheet, or multiple tabs in a web browser? If places can exist side-by-side, how will you indicate which one is the currently active or focused place?

- Can the places be resized, rearranged, opened, closed, or hidden?

- Can the content in different places be interrelated, and if so, how and when will changes to content in one place affect the other places? For instance, in the Eclipse integrated development environment for programmers, if the user enters code containing a syntax error, the error is detected automatically and a notice appears immediately in the *Problems* panel. Or in a spreadsheet, changing a value on one sheet can cause recalculations that affect values on other related sheets.

Navigation map

A navigation map specifies which places exist and what movements from one place to another are permitted. Navigation maps are usually most convenient when represented diagrammatically, but for very large and complex systems, alternative representations such as matrices may be more manageable.

Figure 12-1 is an example of a diagrammatic navigation map for a simple game that offers several screens accessible from a main menu screen.

Navigation maps aren't relevant or useful for all types of application, and there are many cases where drawing a complete map at design time is impractical or impossible. In a wiki application, for instance, users can create an unlimited number of new pages and interlink them however they like.

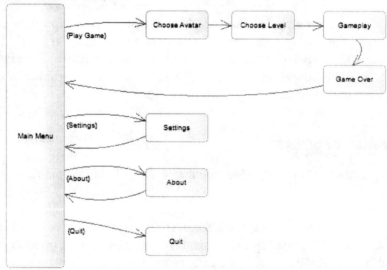

FIGURE 12-1

Navigation mechanisms

The following list explains some of the means by which the user might be able to switch between or navigate to different places. Most applications will use some combination of these.

- *Menus:* Navigation menus on websites direct users to other pages. Pull-down menus in desktop applications often open pop-up dialogs.

- *Hypertext links:* On websites, users can navigate to other pages and sites by means of hypertext links.

- *Buttons:* Clicking or pressing a button or a similar control might cause the application to switch to another place. For example, clicking on a *Next* button will take you to the subsequent step in a wizard, and clicking on a toolbar button might open a pop-up dialog.

- *Hierarchical trees:* Many applications split the display into two panels, with a hierarchical tree control presented in the left-hand panel. By selecting an item in the tree, the right-hand panel refreshes to show the content associated with the selection.

- *Maps:* Some applications might present a clickable or touchable geographical map. A hotel finder, for instance, might show a city map with icons indicating hotels with vacancies.

- *Process flow diagram:* To illustrate the steps in a complex process or workflow, you might present a diagram. For example, Figure 12-2 shows the main screen of QuickBooks, which features a diagram depicting the flow of accounting documents and processes. Clicking an icon in the diagram opens the window appropriate to each type of document or process.

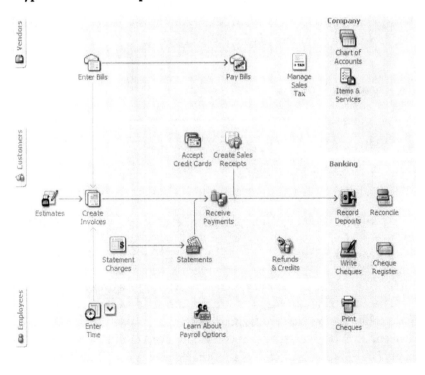

FIGURE 12-2

- *Task flow:* Place changes can be triggered by the completion of a step in a task flow. For example, upon successful completion of a purchase on an e-commerce site, the user is taken to an order confirmation page.

- *Switching:* If multiple places or documents are open at once, the user should be able to switch between them easily and rapidly.

- *Events:* An event triggered by the application itself, or by an input from an external system, could cause a pop-up dialog to appear. A reminder pop-up might appear at a specific time controlled by a timer, or in a stock trading application, an alert might appear when a security's price goes above or below a specified limit.

- *Searching:* Searching for a keyword and presenting a list of clickable matches or documents is a form of navigation. It works well when the user seeks something in particular. It is ineffective for letting the user see what is available in general.

- *Bookmarks and flags:* Content-driven applications, like web browsers and e-book readers, let users bookmark pages or flag specific locations for later access.

- *History:* Some applications, like web browsers, provide a chronological list of recently-accessed places, and offer *Back* and *Forward* buttons for navigating through the history list. Similarly, most Mac desktop applications offer an *Open Recent* menu option allowing rapid access to recently-accessed files.

"You are here" indication

The more places there are in your application, the more important it is to clearly indicate the user's current location. Some common ways of indicating the current location are:

- Conspicuously presenting the title of the place (for instance, in the title bar of a window or dialog, or as a heading at the top of a webpage or screen).

- Highlighting the current location in a visual map or process flow diagram.

- Highlighting the current item or object in a hierarchical tree control.

For websites that organize content in a hierarchical fashion, a **breadcrumb** indicator can work simultaneously as a current-location indicator and as a means of navigation. As shown in the following example from Amazon.com, the breadcrumb indicator at the top lists the categories in the hierarchy that you would need to navigate through in order to get to the final destination, and each of these categories is itself a clickable link allowing access to the page for each category:

De'Longhi EC155 15 BAR Pump Espresso and Cappuccino Maker

DeLonghi EC702 15-Bar-Pump Espresso Maker, Stainless

Mr. Coffee ECM160 4-Cup Steam Espresso Machine, Black

FIGURE 12-3

Searching as a form of navigation

The design of search systems will be discussed in detail in Chapter 16. Searching can be useful as a form of navigation in some circumstances, but it is problematic in the following cases:

- The user doesn't know what is in the repository; or,

- The user is looking for something specific, but doesn't know the right words to describe it; or,

- What is being sought is not easily described in words (for example, the user is seeking a photo with a particular style of composition).

Alternative means of navigating and browsing, such as hierarchical menus, keyword indices, and sitemaps can be useful strategies for allowing users to browse the repository and discover content. Some applications can take advantage of metaphors that simulate real-world situations. For example, a website for a bookstore or library might allow users to view the covers of books in various categories, providing an experience similar to browsing titles on a physical bookshelf. Additionally, some systems might benefit from allowing users to tag content with keywords. Browsing the list of keywords then becomes another way of getting an overview of the repository contents and accessing items.

Designing a common framework for interaction, tasks, and workflow

Many applications are centered around a set of features, tasks, actions, operations, business processes, or use cases that share a similar pattern of interaction. For example:

- A paint program has a toolbar or palette containing various drawing tools. Clicking on a tool selects it, and then the user operates on the canvas with that tool until a different tool is selected.

- A game might have a number of levels, each of which has a different map, but all of the levels have essentially the same gameplay, scoring, and success criteria for moving on to the next level.

- A workflow-driven human resources management system might have different business processes for business events like scheduling job interviews, hiring an employee, recording employee evaluations, or adjusting employee benefits. Each business process can consist of multiple stages or subtasks that require action and approval by different users. Each business process is started by selecting it from a menu, and a business process will have an "active" status until a terminating condition is reached.

If your application has a set of similar tasks or features, you will first want to create a list to keep track of them. You can then design an interaction framework that describes the commonalities of the user interface presentation and behavior for those tasks or features. Some of the issues you should consider include:

- the means by which the tasks are started or triggered (e.g., selection from a menu);

- authorizations, i.e., which tasks can be initiated by which users or groups of users;

- conditions under which tasks can be activated, or cases where tasks may be disabled;

- how the task is ended or deemed to be complete;

- whether the initiation or end of a task changes any statuses or modes;

- whether the completion of the task leads to follow-up tasks; and

- the effects that the task has on the data in the system. For example, upon task completion, the data may be saved persistently, whereas if the task is abandoned or cancelled, the data will not be saved. (These types of considerations can form part of the transaction/persistence concept, discussed in the next section.)

Designing the framework for interactions ensures that you understand how your application will fundamentally behave. It helps ensure consistency across similar tasks, so that users can perceive patterns and form correct mental models. By documenting the commonalities amongst the tasks in the framework, it also saves you from having to re-document the same aspects for each individual task when creating designs and writing specifications. The framework will also be critical for helping the development team design and build the technical platform or framework with which the various tasks can be implemented.

Thinking about transactions and persistence

Most applications deal with data that needs to be stored persistently — that is, saved — so that it can be accessed later. A **persistence concept** or **transaction concept** is the design, at the user-interface level, of how the saving and visibility of data works in your application. To help us understand what's involved in interaction design for persistence and transactions, let's first look at how data is saved in two typical classes of applications: document-oriented desktop applications, and multi-user web and client-server applications.

Document-oriented desktop applications

For document-oriented desktop applications like word processors and spreadsheets, documents are usually saved as individual files on a disk.

When a user is working with a such an application, there is a copy of the document stored in the working memory of the user's computer. As the user edits the document, the copy in working memory is modified, and it will no longer match the copy on disk. By saving the document, the copy on disk will be refreshed so that its contents match the copy in working memory. But if the user makes changes to the document and then closes the document or the application without saving the document, then any changes will be lost.

Most people with computing experience are familiar with this model. You can indicate that your application uses this model by following standard operating system or platform conventions. Usually, for Mac and Windows applications, that means that there should be *Save* and *Save As...* commands under the *File* menu, and on Windows, there is typically a *Save* icon in the toolbar. On Mac OS X, a black dot appears in the red "Close

Window" button whenever unsaved changes are present (see Figure 12-4), and this dot disappears after the document has been saved. On Windows, some applications place an asterisk next to the document title in the window's title bar when unsaved changes are present.

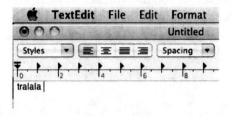

FIGURE 12-4

Some usability specialists argue that the need to know about the separation between working memory and persistent storage is a **leaky abstraction** — an underlying implementation detail of the technology that is exposed to the user, creating an unnecessary mental burden.

The *Canon Cat* was a unique word processing system designed by Jef Raskin in the 1980s that hid the distinction between working memory and persistent storage. No *Save* command was offered because the system automatically synchronized all changes with the copy on disk. The popular word processing application *Scrivener* similarly saves all changes automatically every few seconds, meaning that users never have to worry about explicitly saving their work. Diverting from the conventional way of doing things can initially cause users confusion, though, and so *Scrivener* still offers a *Save* command in the *File* menu for convenience, even though it's never really necessary.

Multi-user web and client-server applications

For most web applications and client-server applications, data is usually stored in a database. A database system allows data to be managed in a structured way, and permits many different users to access the data simultaneously.

In applications that are backed by a database, when a user creates, edits, or deletes data in the system, the changes are accumulated into units called **transactions**. If other users of the system retrieve data from the database while the first user's transaction is still in progress, the other users will not be able to see these changes; only the first user can see his or her "local" changes. But when the software issues a "commit" command for the first user's transaction, the transaction is ended, and the user's accumulated pending changes are saved permanently to the database so that other users of the system can see

138

those changes.

If instead a "rollback" command is issued, the transaction is also ended, but all of the pending changes for that user's transaction are cancelled, and the database is not updated; other users see no changes in the data in the database.

Applications that rely on databases should generally hide the technical concepts of transactions, commits, and rollbacks from the user. This hiding can be done by aligning the start and end of transactions with places in the user interface where events or flows start and end. Database-specific terminology should also be replaced with terminology that is more familiar to the user. For example, we can imagine that when a dialog box such as a *Properties* dialog is opened, a new transaction will be started. If the user closes the dialog or presses the *Cancel* button, then the transaction will be rolled back and any changes the user had made in the dialog will be lost. If the user presses the *OK* button, the user's changes in the dialog will be committed to the database.

For multi-user systems, you also need to think about what happens when two users try to edit the same information records simultaneously.

Imagine a situation where two users are attempting to make changes to the address information on file for a particular customer. The original address on file is "123 Main Street". User A opens the address record and starts changing "123 Main Street" to "456 First Ave.", while seconds later, User B opens the same address record and starts changing "123 Main Street" to "789 Second Ave." If User A presses *OK* to save the changes, and then User B presses *OK* shortly afterwards, what happens to the data on file? There are a couple of theoretical possibilities:

1. User A's changes get saved, but then User B's changes overwrite User A's changes. So the address on file at the end is "789 Second Ave."

2. User A's changes get saved, but User B's changes are ignored (or an error message appears) because User A's changes have invalidated the data that User B was working with. So the address on file at the end is "123 Main Street".

Neither of these is particularly satisfying, as both users may think that their changes have been saved, but one user will have had their changes overwritten or lost without their knowledge.

One solution to this issue is to use some form of **record locking**: When User A opens the customer record, the system **locks** that record, so that if User B attempts to open the same record, User B receives a message that the record is locked and unavailable for editing. When User A commits or rolls back his or her changes, then the lock is removed and the other users can edit the record again.

One problem with locks is that if User A leaves his or her terminal and goes home, or if User A's application or operating system crashes, the lock might be stuck in place, preventing other users from editing the record until an administrator can intervene.

In many applications, you may wish to allow multiple users to *view* the same record simultaneously, but only one user at a time should be able to *edit* the data. This raises the question of whether users who are viewing a record should be notified when the record they are viewing has been changed by another user. If there is no notification and if the display is not automatically refreshed, the user will be looking at **stale data** that no longer matches the current state of the database, and this may or may not be a problem depending on the nature of the application.

Collaborative web-based applications where users work together on editing the same document can present many challenges like these, and it can take some creative thinking to find usable and non-intrusive solutions to avoid or manage simultaneous editing conflicts.

Designing and documenting a transaction and persistence concept

We've seen that an application's usability can be impacted by how persistence is presented via the user interface and interaction design, and by how problems like multi-user editing conflicts are handled. Therefore, explicitly designing how these aspects will work from a user's standpoint is a good idea for data-driven applications.

To design a transaction and persistence concept, you need to answer the following questions:

- What types of data validations take place, and when are these validations performed? How are errors and warnings presented?

- Can data or documents be saved when validation errors exist or when mandatory fields are empty?

- At what points in the application can data be saved? How and when can any changes be lost (intentionally or unintentionally)?

- If the system uses transactions, where and when do the transactions begin and end?

- Does the application save data automatically, or does it rely on the user to give some form of *Save* or *Commit* command? Are controls such as *Save* menu options or toolbar buttons prominently visible, and is it clear to the user how and when to use them?

- How is the user interface structured to help users understand whether data is in a saved or unsaved state?

- If the applications saves one or more types of documents to disk, what file types will be supported, and what default file extensions will these document types have? Will standard data exchange formats be used (e.g., can reports be saved into formats such as PDF or RTF?), or will proprietary file formats be used?

You'll often need to clarify some of these questions with the technical architects and developers in your project, as the technology framework being used can sometimes influence how some of these aspects will have to work. At the same time, just because the technology handles some of these aspects in a certain way at the technical implementation level, doesn't mean that all of those details necessarily need to be exposed directly to the user. Whenever possible, create the design that is clearest and easiest for the user, and then build the system to support that way of working.

Designing the application-wide visual design

In most applications, most of your pages, screens, or windows will share a common visual design. For example, most websites and web applications will have a page template with a banner, a navigation menu, a content area, a footer, and so on, and this template will be shared by all pages on the website. Desktop applications similarly have a basic structure with a window title, menu bar, toolbars, scrollbars, and so on. No matter what kind of application you're working with, there will also be stylistic commonalities throughout, such as standard fonts for text and headings, and a standard color scheme.

As part of the interaction concept, it is valuable to create an initial design for this overall template or framework for the visual appearance. This is especially recommended in larger teams with multiple designers and developers, because it can be difficult to keep everyone producing designs that are consistent with each other.

To do this, you might consider creating a **style guide** which describes the visual framework in terms of visual components, styles, guidelines, and rules. Style guides will be covered in more detail in Chapter 15.

Alternatively, a visual design concept can be expressed through a high-fidelity prototype. A prototype and a style guide together can be the most effective combination, because the prototype then serves as a concrete demonstration of the style guide's guidelines and rules in action.

The visual design framework should involve only the high-level, common features of the general screen design and anticipated task flows. The detailed design of specific individual screens or pages or flows for specific tasks will then fit into the visual design framework provided by the style guide, and the detailed work of specifying the appearance and behavior of those individual pages and flows can be done at a later stage.

The visual design framework is never set in stone and can be expected to evolve over the life of the project. Nevertheless, it is valuable to produce a rough draft at an early stage of the project.

We will learn more about visual design in Chapter 13.

13

Designing the visual appearance

Interaction design can be seen as specifying the *appearance* and the *behavior* of a system:

- The **appearance** (or **presentation**) describes what controls, content, and/or data are shown, how these elements are shown, and the overall general visual design.

- The **behavior** is how the user interface reacts and what the application or website does when you operate the controls or otherwise interact with the interface.

In this chapter, we'll examine designing the presentation of a user interface. Putting some effort into getting the presentation right is important for a lot of reasons.

The visual design of your product – the layout, colors, fonts, and so on – differentiates it from other products, and is one of the first things your users will notice when they encounter your product, so it contributes to users' first impressions. If your product looks professional, it will inspire more trust and confidence.

Beyond first impressions, the presentation of the user interface gives the user the means to discover and activate the functionality that your application or website provides. Functions might be activated by picking menu entries, clicking on icons in a toolbar, typing commands, directly manipulating visual objects (e.g., painting on a canvas in a paint program, or moving a spaceship in a game), or other means.

As we learned in Chapter 10, making your application's possible actions and functions *visible* is important, especially for new users who are learning how to use the application. For example, users looking for a search function will be able to find it if there is an appropriate icon in a toolbar, or a text box labelled *Search*, whereas if a search can only be activated by pressing a keystroke combination such as Ctrl-F7, it's quite likely that most users will never discover it. But there are trade-offs to consider. If your application provides a great number of functions, putting hundreds of confusing buttons or icons in several rows of toolbars might be overwhelming. Presenting these instead as items in cascading pull-down menus might clean up the clutter, and would give the user textual descriptions instead of icons to decipher – but it will take longer to navigate through menus to activate a function. And power users might want keyboard shortcuts so that they don't have to reach for the mouse.

Another aspect of appearance is the **layout** of screens or pages. The layout of elements and controls can be used to explicitly or implicitly communicate relationships between entities. For example, grouping a set of things together in one area of the page will give a visual clue that suggests that those things are logically related. And if there's a header over a block of text or a set of fields, you'd expect the all the things under that header to relate to what the header says. Careful attention to layout can make understanding your application easier, whereas sloppy and inconsistent layouts can cause unnecessary confusion.

Understanding how people process visual information

To better understand how to create effective screen and page designs, let's take a look at how people perceive and interpret visual information.

How do people scan and read pages?

Visual designers have long been interested in figuring out how to guide a reader's eyes across the printed page or computer screen. For example, artists creating posters use emphasis and positioning to draw your attention to a headline. Cartoonists carefully draw cartoons so that you notice the characters and read the speech bubbles in a certain order, and without this, the jokes might lose their impact.

By laying out elements on the page in certain ways, you can affect the order in which people will notice the elements and how long they will spend looking at them. For software designers, if you know that people will tend to scan a page in a certain way, you can design your page to accommodate those usage patterns, by putting relevant information in the places where people are likely to look.

So, let's begin by examining how readers read text on a page.

If a reader is reading a book, such as a novel, where every page consists of rows of text (we'll assume there are no illustrations), then the reader will start by looking at the first word in the top-left corner of the page, scan across the line from left to right to read the words, and then skip to the beginning of the next line. The reader will again scan left to right to read the line, skip to the next line, and continue in this pattern until the bottom of the page is reached. (And, yes, in languages like Arabic and Hebrew, readers would read right-to-left instead.)

However, when the eye scans across a line of the text, it's not actually a smooth movement as you might expect. Rather than moving smoothly in a line, the eyes' focus instead jumps rapidly between spots on the page, called **fixation points**. These jumps are called **saccades**. The brain doesn't receive any visual information during saccades, but it's able to stitch together the images received at the fixation points, and the brain perceives it as "seeing in a line".

The area that you can see clearly at each fixation point — i.e., the area that you can focus on — is called your **foveal vision**, and that area is surprisingly small: it's only about two degrees of your visual field, or about twice the width of your thumb if you stick your thumb out at arm's length. Try holding your arm out straight and put your thumb on a paragraph of text on the page or on your screen right now. Look at your thumb, and without looking away, try to see how many words on the screen you can clearly distinguish around your thumb. Your area of focus is pretty limited; you're still able to perceive the rest of the screen in your peripheral vision, but you can't see those other parts of the screen clearly. You can only resolve text in the narrow area that you're focusing on.

For page layouts that are more complex and heterogeneous than solid blocks of text, it's more difficult to say exactly how readers' eyes will move across the page, and of course, it will differ for each reader, but we can try to make some generalizations.

Traditionally, visual designers have believed that when readers look at a complex document like a newspaper, they generally first get an overall impression by scanning the page in a Z-shaped pattern. They start in the upper-left corner, read the title of the newspaper across the top, and then, beginning at the upper-right corner, they gradually skim over the page in a roughly diagonal line until they reach the lower-left corner. Then they skim across to the right, ending in the lower-right corner. Then readers will go back and focus on whatever interests them.

However, if there is something particularly flashy or eye-catching on the page — a large color photo, or a bold, interesting headline — the reader will probably look at that first, or perhaps the reader may begin a Z-shaped scan, but interrupt it to look at the interesting bits. Someone specifically looking for some particular detail will also probably search through the page in a different pattern than someone who is just browsing.

To better understand how people look at visual information, researchers have conducted eye-tracking studies using specialized cameras and software that can identify what a user is looking at on a screen. The software can then play back the **scanpath** — the series of fixations and saccades — to show what areas of the screen the participant has looked at and how long they have spent gazing at each fixation point. While the scanpaths of individual users can vary quite a bit, if you ask a number of users to look at the same webpage or screen, you can combine all of the scanpaths to create aggregate **heatmap** diagrams that show where users, on average, spend the most time looking.

Probably the most detailed and best-documented eye-tracking studies are those included in the book *Eyetracking Web Usability* (Nielsen and Pernice, 2009). They discovered some interesting findings:

- For most websites, rather than following the traditional Z-shaped scanning pattern, most users follow a roughly F-shaped pattern. They read across the top, and then go down the page and read lines (or partial lines) of text left to right. But users are, in general, more likely to read complete paragraphs or lines of text near the top of the screen, whereas they tend to lose interest and just briefly scan the text near the bottom of the page. And then, upon reaching the bottom of the screen, users often apparently make an additional quick scan down the left-hand edge of the page (especially if there is a sidebar with links). The upper-left corner receives the most attention, and the lower-right corner receives the least.

- Graphics, and especially photographic images, will attract attention, but only when they are a relevant and integral part of the content. People seems to be able to quickly judge whether images are just decorative stock photos, and such superficial photos get very little attention after the first glance. A majority of users pretty much completely ignore banner ads on websites; when there was a banner ad at the top of the webpage, most users started their F-shaped scans below the ads, where the content begins.

- Users tend to ignore elements that are repeated on multiple pages. Once they've seen the logo or navigation bar at the top of the page, they don't look there again unless they need to.

Something that I haven't seen discussed in eye-tracking studies is the degree of focus of the viewer's eyes. I personally find that I sometimes scan pages by slightly defocusing my eyes, which makes the page look a little blurry, but enables you to perceive the whole layout at once, somewhat like viewing the page from ten feet away. I don't believe that eye-tracking equipment can detect the degree of focus, only the direction of gaze.

Let's now turn to examining some of the key principles that explain how people interpret visual elements and layouts. A key set of such principles are the *Gestalt Laws of Perception*.

The Gestalt Laws of Perception

The **Gestalt Laws of Perception** help explain how humans perceive and make sense of visual information. As user interface designers, the laws are interesting to us because we can exploit them to create visual layouts and representations that help communicate concepts and relationships that exist in our underlying conceptual model for the application.

Gestalt (pronounced *ge-SHTALT*) is a German word that means roughly means "shape", "form", "essence", or "whole". Gestalt psychology is based on the idea that, when the human mind perceives the world, it seeks to recognize some kind of structure or order. Specifically, the **Gestalt effect** suggests that, when we are presented with a complex visual image, our minds attempt to recognize coherent, whole forms, rather than individually perceiving all of the smaller constituent parts that make up the image.

That might sound pretty heavy and abstract, so let's take a closer look to understand what this really means.

Max Wertheimer's paper *Laws of Organization in Perceptual Forms* (1923) stated a number of principles or "laws" that describe how the mind tends to perceive visual information:

Law of Prägnanz

The basic law, from which the others are derived, is the *Law of Prägnanz*. *Prägnanz* might be roughly and imperfectly translated as *conciseness* or *simplicity*.

The Law of Prägnanz is a bit like Occam's Razor. **Occam's Razor** states that the simplest explanations for a state of affairs tend to be more likely to be correct than complicated and convoluted explanations that rely on unproven assumptions or special conditions. (For example, "an alien stole my homework" is probably an unlikely excuse for why an assignment wasn't handed in, whereas "I just didn't do my homework" is a simpler and likelier explanation, as it doesn't presume the existence of extraterrestrials.)

The Law of Prägnanz says that when the mind tries to interpret a visual scene, it will try to interpret it in the simplest, most concise, and most easily recognizable way. In particular, the mind will try to perceive the scene as a whole rather than as a sum of parts. For example, when you see the following illustration…

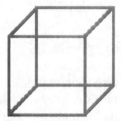

FIGURE 13-1

…you probably recognize it as a cube. You don't think of it as twelve separate lines, nor do you think of it as four parallel horizontal lines, four parallel vertical lines, and four parallel diagonal lines.

In trying to explain how the mind tries to perceive complex scenes, Wertheimer elucidated the following additional laws that contribute to the Law of Prägnanz. We'll examine each one, using examples relevant to user interface design.

Law of proximity

Items that are located close together tend to be perceived as being a single group. The items in that group are considered to be distinct and different from items located further away.

For example, in the following image, we seem to perceive three separate groups:

FIGURE 13-2

And in the following image, some of these dots appear to be arranged in rows, and others in columns.

o o o o o o o o o o o   o   o   o   o   o

FIGURE 13-3

It's due to their *proximity*. The distance between the dots making up each row or column is less than the distance between a dot in one row or column and the nearest dot in the next row or column.

Applying the law of proximity to user interface design, consider this data-entry form:

Username

First Name

Last Name

E-mail

Phone

FIGURE 13-4

Conceptually, each label matches up with a corresponding text-entry field. And yet the labels are so far away from the text-entry fields that the labels appear to form their own group, and the fields appear to form another group. The connection between each label and its corresponding field isn't as obvious as it could be. One way to fix this is to move the labels and fields closer together so that we're emphasizing the horizontal pairs of labels and fields rather than the two columns:

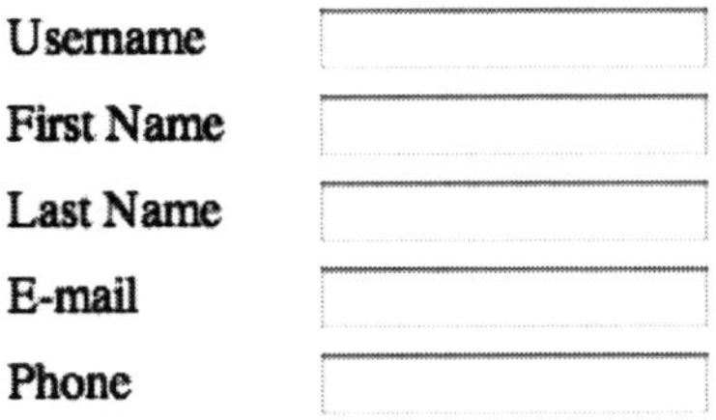

Username

First Name

Last Name

E-mail

Phone

FIGURE 13-5

Law of similarity

Visual items that share some property or attribute are perceived as belonging together, whereas items with differing properties or attributes are perceived as belonging to different groups.

For example, in the following image, you can probably detect three groups, even though the items in those groups aren't in proximity to each other. (Note that the triangles are red, the circles are green, and the squares are grey.)

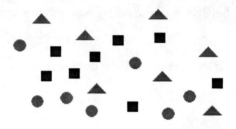

FIGURE 13-6

This is the law of similarity at work with two attributes: shape and color. The red triangles are easily detectable as a grouping because they share the same shape and color. The red triangles are distinguishable from the green circles and the grey squares because those items differ in those two attributes.

An example from UI design comes from file managers in operating systems: Usually, all of the files of the same type (like MP3 files) are decorated with the same icon, to provide a visual indication that those files share something in common. In the following example on a Mac, the icons aren't different enough that you can instantly tell that they're different (they all have the same basic "curled page" shape and they all have a bit of blue in them), so the effect is not quite as strong as it could be:

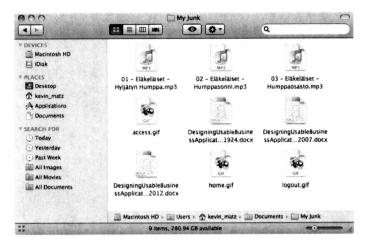

FIGURE 13-7

However, in the next image, the "highlighting" decoration on selected items easily differentiates the group of selected items from the group of unselected items:

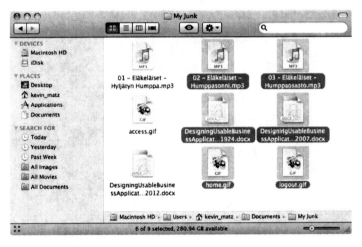

FIGURE 13-8

Returning to the data-entry form example, if we wanted to improve the form without moving the groups closer together, we could also try making the pairings more explicit by making sure that each label and field share an attribute, like the background color:

Username	
First Name	
Last Name	
E-mail	
Phone	

FIGURE 13-9

Law of continuation

Visual items that appear to be a continuation of a preceding sequence or line of similar items are perceived as belonging together. As well, once your eye begins following the line or sequence, it will continue doing so until something else catches your attention. For example, the icons on this Eclipse splash screen are arranged to a form a curve that your eye is likely to follow:

FIGURE 13-10

Law of closure

Lines (or visual elements that are repeated to form lines) are more likely to be perceived together as a common visual unit if they appear to form the outline or "closure" of a surface or shape, even if that outline is not complete. The mind fills in any gaps in incomplete shapes, to achieve closure in the form of a familiar shape.

In the following classic example, we perceive the image to be a circle, even though part of the circle is missing:

152

FIGURE 13-11

Our minds fill in the missing gap because the explanation "it's a circle with a small piece missing" is simpler and more satisfying to grasp than the explanation "it's an arc spanning about 320 degrees".

This law might be applied to logos and other decorative artwork that might appear on webpages or splash screens to catch the user's attention. Incomplete or cropped shapes and forms can create visual interest, because the mind has to do a bit of work to fill in the missing information to visualize the complete shape. For example, the logo in Figure 13-12 crops a geometric flower shape, and it's somewhat eye-catching because you have to mentally complete the pattern to achieve closure.

FIGURE 13-12

Law of common fate

Visual elements moving together in the same direction simultaneously tend to be perceived as a group.

For example, in Microsoft Windows or Mac OS, if you select a number of icons and then drag-and-drop them, partially-transparent copies of all of the selected icons move together as a group:

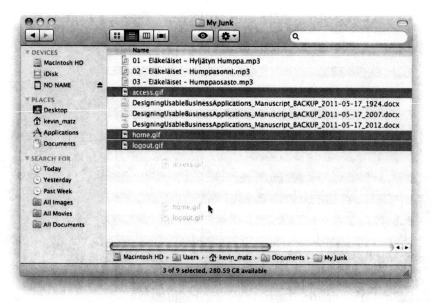

FIGURE 13-13

Law of good continuation (or "good Gestalt")

Line segments that are smooth continuations of each other are perceived as the same line, even in the case of intersections of multiple line segments.

For example, when you see this figure...

FIGURE 13-14

...you probably perceive it as the two straight lines crossing:

FIGURE 13-15

154

You are unlikely to perceive it as two angles meeting, even though that is a possibility as well:

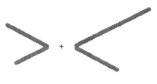

FIGURE 13-16

Your mind knows from experience that the "two straight lines crossing" is more plausible.

Admittedly, I can't think of a good application of this law to UI design, but I've included it for completeness.

Beyond Wertheimer's laws, additional related laws have been proposed, such as:

Law of common region (Palmer, 1992)

Visual items situated together in demarcated (bordered) regions are perceived as belonging together.

For example, Figure 13-17 shows a *Print* dialog from Microsoft Word. The various controls are grouped together and contained in frames. It's clear that all of the controls within the *Copies* frame belong together and relate to controlling the number of copies.

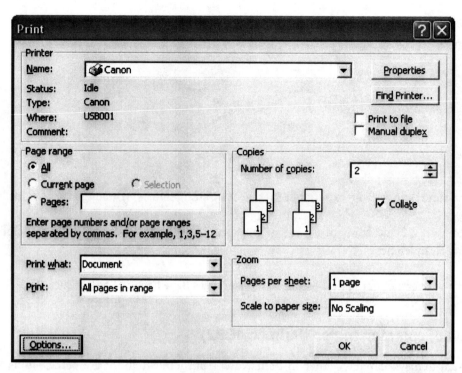

FIGURE 13-17

Law of synchrony (Palmer and Levitin, 1998)

Visual items that change at the same time will tend to be perceived as belonging together as a unit.

Law of connected elements (Palmer and Rock, 1994)

If items are joined together to form a compound item, that compound item will tend to be perceived as a single object.

Summary

The Gestalt Laws of Perception help us understand how people interpret visual designs. In designing user interfaces, applying these laws can often help us to reinforce our underlying conceptual models. For example, we can intentionally group related fields together on the screen to indicate that they are related, or use similar icons or other decorations to provide visual clues that certain objects belong to a certain class.

156

Visual attributes

Visual elements are the things you put on your page or screen. For a software application, this can include user interface controls such as icons, buttons, text fields, checkboxes, drop-down lists, menus, and so on. But it can also include text, images, and organizational or decorative elements like borders, lines, and separators.

Visual attributes are *properties* of visual elements — in other words, the different ways that you can *style* the visual elements on the page.

In designing the visual style for your application or website, you'll need to decide on a system of arrangement of visual elements, combined with a consistent way of styling those elements using visual attributes.

Elements with similar function and meaning should usually be styled the same way. But you can also selectively use attributes to create *contrast*. **Contrast** is an intentional and immediately recognizable visual difference between two elements. Contrast is eye-catching and can be selectively employed to highlight or draw attention to a particular element, or to provide clues that two elements are different in some conceptual way.

Here are some of the main visual attributes you need to be aware of:

Size

The most instantly noticeable visual attribute of all is **size**. We can't help but notice when one element is bigger than another, and, all other things being equal, our eyes will usually be drawn towards the biggest thing on a page first. So size can be intentionally used to draw attention to something.

For example, book designers have for centuries used **dropcaps** — like in the "E" in the paragraph below — to help direct the eye to the beginning of long blocks of text (which are not always visually exciting):

Em ium accatibus acea sin consedi doluptur, totat fuga. Uga. La sumqui quostrunt offic testiis es ne nobitibus ni nobisquiant illa aut placere doluptus, opta distium inum quia aboreptae init excesed quibear chicitate ne nus etur rem ea aut iumquatem sitatii ssequae es am quatio ma sa venis doluptatur sitam, officaeribus expliquid ut explia nam ape mi, inctur ad molorum fugitas eatatur? Qui ratiat delita pelitiandis que ni occae. Aximil et ut quis quam, nobist, quias si vidi ate con con corecabo. Ut omniasp ero- repudit ditat est lab ipsam aute nimi, nobit, apid min nestem. Duciatur animus, quam, cumet offic te repudi tet vel ipsanda dolenes dolum non cum num quia volut volorep taspell amendae conse nonseque dolorrorpori volupti onecaep erorro offici blam re, venim elibus dolupta porrorum vit autas dolut est dunt, odit, ut in evenisita quiae. Abor sitaes moluptatem iligendandae quae. Et apiendandis sim et am andam il eos sam quis a de solore, quiatur? Qui ratiat delita pelitiandis que ni occae. Aximil et ut quis quam.

FIGURE 13-18

If an element is bigger than other surrounding elements, the contrast in relative size makes the bigger element visually dominant, meaning that the bigger element tends to be perceived as being more important than the nearby smaller elements.

For example, here, despite not being able to see the contents of the panels, we would generally assume that the big center panel is the most important on the basis of its size:

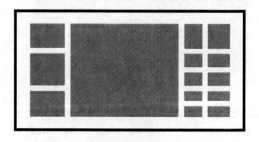

FIGURE 13-19

The relative size of elements can be used to communicate the intended relative importance of those elements. So if you expect that certain features will be used more frequently, you might make the buttons for those features larger than the buttons for lesser-used features, or devote more screen real estate to the parts of the screen related to those features.

Users may also have their own expectations for what is important and not, and they could be annoyed if seemingly irrelevant things are taking up too much screen real estate. For example, a time-and-date clock in the corner of an accounting program should be small because, while convenient, it has little to do with the main task of the application. However, in a "chyron" system for overlaying graphics onto live television broadcasts, a time clock can be important for synchronization, and so making it large and prominent would be justifiable.

Size contrasts can also be used as a highlighting technique. For example, in this particular view of the Mac OS dock, the currently selected item is biggest:

FIGURE 13-20

Color

After size, **color** is generally regarded as the next most immediately noticeable attribute. Color, when applied carefully and appropriately, can be used to attract attention and guide the eye. Color can also work very well for suggesting importance: brighter, more intense colors tend to suggest more importance and urgency than duller, muted colors.

Color can also be used to suggest similarities and differences. Elements sharing identical colors are perceived as belonging to the same group, whereas elements with contrasting colors are perceived as belonging to different groups.

Colors can also have implied meanings, and if your product will be used internationally, care should be taken when choosing colors, as the implied meanings of colors can vary between different cultures. For instance, in Western countries, red is often used for signalling "danger" or "stop", whereas in China, red can connote happiness and good fortune.

Shape

We can perceive and differentiate the outlines of shapes very easily. We can quite rapidly tell the difference between squares, circles, and triangles.

You can draw attention to one object if it has a different outline shape than the objects surrounding it – for example, a round or a pointy angular shape in a sea of boxes:

FIGURE 13-21

And as we saw earlier in Figure 13-7, the icons in the Mac Finder window all had very similar general outline shapes and colorings, which made it more difficult to quickly tell the difference between them.

Direction and angularity

Page layouts are often arranged using a grid system that helps keep things aligned. Elements like text, lines, or graphics that are set at an angle create **visual tension** by breaking the traditional rules of grid alignment. Traditional design wisdom says that angular elements are perceived as being unconventional and edgy, so conservative, respectable business applications like banking websites will generally tend to avoid them, but they are often suitable in contexts such as entertainment and game applications.

Weight

Weight refers to the thickness of lines:

FIGURE 13-22

When applied to text, weight refers to the thickness of the lines of the letterforms. Bold text has a heavier weight — more "heft" — than regular text. Many typefaces are available in families, where the letterforms have the same basic shapes but have different weights. Most famous is Helvetica:

160

Helvetica Neue UltraLight
Helvetica Neue Light
Helvetica Neue Regular
Helvetica Neue Medium
Helvetica Neue Bold

FIGURE 13-23

Using the same typeface but using different weights can create contrast:

FIGURE 13-24

Text styling

Apart from size and weight, further attributes for text are stylistic variations and decorations like italics and underlining.

Texture

Texture refers to the appearance of the surfaces of elements so that, if they were actually touchable, might feel rough, or smooth, or concave or convex, etc. Panels and buttons might look like they're made of shiny brushed metal, or illuminated plastic, or semi-transparent glass; a page background might look like paper or wood. The so-called "Web 2.0" look relies a lot on illumination, reflections, gradients, and shading effects to create a more sophisticated, "photorealistic" texture that stands out more than simple blocks of plain colors.

In the following illustration, on the left, buttons from Mac OS and Windows 7 are shown; these look like raised, convex, clear plastic buttons that look very pressable. In the center, a scrollbar from Java Swing's (old) Metal look-and-feel has a grippy tactile texture that makes you want to touch it and drag it up and down. On the right is an example of a novelty background texture for websites (courtesy of *allfreebackgrounds.com*).

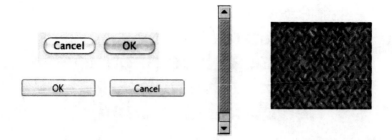

FIGURE 13-25

Textures can give your user interface a unique look-and-feel, but for business applications, you probably don't want to get too carried away; it's usually best to stick to more conservative styling. Novelty textures, like UI components appearing to be carved out of wood or stone, might help give an immersive ambiance to a game, however.

Note that graphic designers also use the word *texture* to refer to the overall visual effect of a block of text. If you look at a block of text and squint or defocus your eyes until you can no longer distinguish the actual words, you may see a texture emerge. If you were to imagine that the text were raised off the page, and you could close your eyes and rub your fingertip over it, then a block of text set in Times New Roman (upper left) would probably feel different to the touch than a block set in Helvetica (upper right), or Times New Roman Italic (lower left), or Gill Sans Regular (lower right):

Enihilluptas acesece rchillabo. Nam, volupturem. Itae vid moloris tibusda que et abo. Agnatem eum excerias qui dipsand ucipsamus alitatia alictibus non remqui odi ullaci consequi ullorest audic te veligniminus ducia nis solorehendam verum sundaerat facia delesto tatium volor re mos pa quis eliquo quatus audis que poreium etur, con con exped untest, il il minusantiam endi dolupit que porporum est laborio esti odit volum sitatur aut ut vel etus del inciende nullenim audit, sunt aut quam, id ut prae consed magni incillit haribusapis ut vollicit qui coquilla.

Enihilluptas acesece rchillabo. Nam, volupturem. Itae vid moloris tibusda que et abo. Agnatem eum excerias qui dipsand ucipsamus alitatia alictibus non remqui odi ullaci consequi ullorest audic te veligniminus ducia nis solorehendam verum sundaerat facia delesto tatium volor re mos pa quis eliquo quatus audis que poreium etur, con con exped untest, il il minusantiam endi dolupit que porporum est laborio esti odit volum sitatur aut ut vel etus del inciende nullenim audit, sunt aut quam, id ut prae consed magni incil-

Enihilluptas acesece rchillabo. Nam, volupturem. Itae vid moloris tibusda que et abo. Agnatem eum excerias qui dipsand ucipsamus alitatia alictibus non remqui odi ullaci consequi ullorest audic te veligniminus ducia nis solorehendam verum sundaerat facia delesto tatium volor re mos pa quis eliquo quatus audis que poreium etur, con con exped untest, il il minusantiam endi dolupit que porporum est laborio esti odit volum sitatur aut ut vel etus del inciende nullenim audit, sunt aut quam, id ut prae consed magni incillit haribusapis ut vollicit qui coquilla.

Enihilluptas acesece rchillabo. Nam, volupturem. Itae vid moloris tibusda que et abo. Agnatem eum excerias qui dipsand ucipsamus alitatia alictibus non remqui odi ullaci consequi ullorest audic te veligniminus ducia nis solorehendam verum sundaerat facia delesto tatium volor re mos pa quis eliquo quatus audis que poreium etur, con con exped untest, il il minusantiam endi dolupit que porporum est laborio esti odit volum sitatur aut ut vel etus del inciende nullenim audit, sunt aut quam, id ut prae consed magni incillit haribusapis ut vollicit qui coquilla. Ik ben verpleegster uit

FIGURE 13-26

Surrounding space

Humans place value on **space**, and things that take up more space than necessary tend to be perceived as being important and valuable. Surrounding space can thus be one of the most effective attributes for creating contrast. If an element is in a region that's tightly packed with other elements, it will not stand out. But if that element is surrounded by generous whitespace, we'll tend to believe it must be either special or valuable to deserve all that space.

How to build a visual hierarchy to express relationships between page elements

The underlying structure of a page's layout can be understood as a **visual hierarchy**, where some visual elements on the page are conceptually *subordinate* to others. The visual hierarchy helps guide the user's eye through the page, and aids users in interpreting the content of the page by giving clues to the relationships amongst the elements.

Take this sample webpage for example:

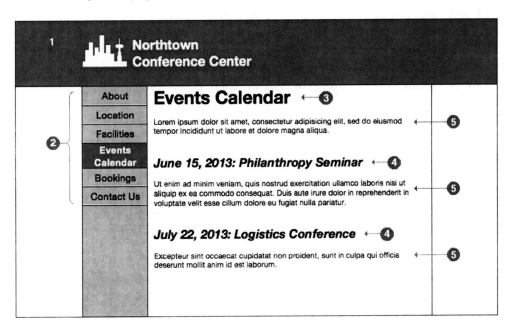

Figure 13-27

The banner (1) is the highest element in the hierarchy of this page. The banner, and the logo within the banner, tell the viewer that everything on the page is associated with the site named in the logo. Everything below the banner and logo are subordinate to these elements.

The navigation bar (2) on the left-hand side of the page comes second in the visual hierarchy.

The main content panel's heading, "Events Calendar" (3), which describes the contents that follow, forms the third element in the visual hierarchy.

The two subheadings (4) are subordinate to the main heading, so they come next in the visual hierarchy.

Finally, the sections of body text (5) are subordinate to their respective headings. These come last in the visual hierarchy.

When scanning the page, the viewer's eye will tend to look first at the banner, then move to either the navigation sidebar or the main heading. While the viewer may read the content under the main heading from top to bottom, it is likely that the viewer's eye will be caught by the subheadings first, and then the viewer's eye may go back to read the body text.

Why is the viewer likely to scan the page in this way? The visual hierarchy has been intentionally designed to express the relationships between the elements on the page, and the elements' relative importance, and this has been achieved through:

- the choice of visual *attributes* of the elements on the page, and

- the relative *positioning* of the elements.

Let's now take a closer look at using attributes and positioning to create a visual hierarchy.

Attributes

Visual attributes, as we've explored previously in this chapter, are the general stylistic properties of visual elements on the page, such as size, shape, color, texture, and direction.

Visual elements that are either conceptually similar, belong to the same category, or have equal importance, should generally share the same attributes, whereas elements that are intended to be different should have one or more contrasting attributes.

Most crucially for creating a visual hierarchy, if one element is intended to be stronger than or superior to another element, then the attributes of the elements should be chosen to reflect that fact. For example, if you have a list or a menu, then all of the entries belong to the same class or category of elements, and so they should be styled consistently with the same attributes. But the heading that sits atop the list serves a different function. It describes or summarizes the contents of the list or menu, and so it should be styled with contrasting attributes that emphasize its dominance. The heading might be larger or bolder, or it may take a different typeface or color.

Contrast is weak when the elements being contrasted are only slightly different. When two elements differ only slightly, it can often look like the difference is accidental. Strong contrast is produced when the differences are clearly intentional. To create intentional contrast between two elements, the general guideline is to make sure that the elements differ in at least *two* ways. In other words, at least *two attributes* should be different between the elements. As surrounding space is considered to be an attribute as well, leaving a gap of whitespace between two elements can count as one of the differences.

Figure 13-28 demonstrates some examples of weak contrast and strong contrast between a heading and a list of items:

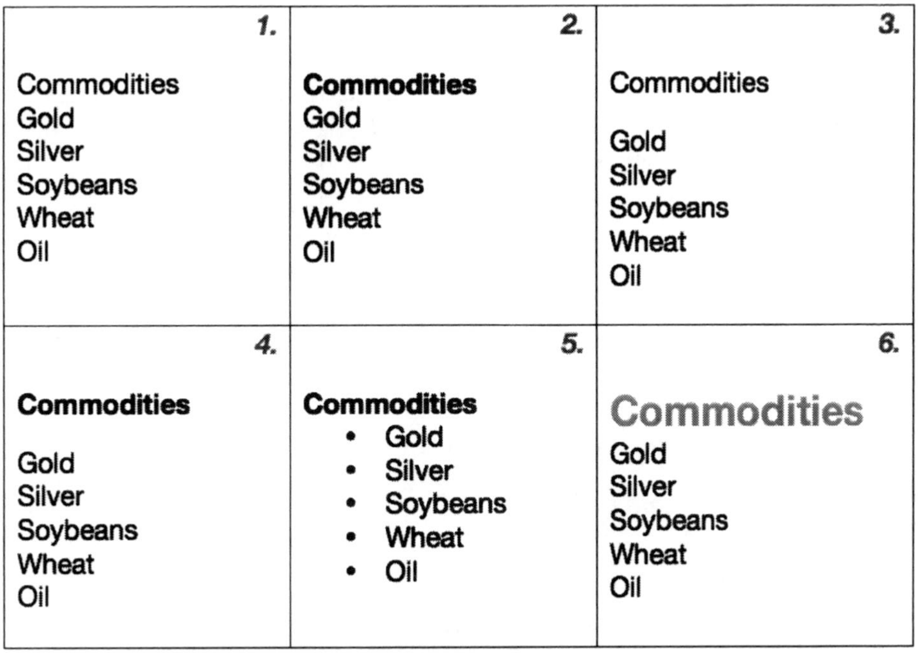

FIGURE 13-28

In example (1), there are no differences between the heading "Commodities" and the entries in the list, so it is not visually distinguishable as a heading at all.

Example (2) is better — the heading is in bold type — but the difference still does not stand out strongly.

Example (3) places a gap between the heading and the list. While this is also better than (1), it is still not satisfying, as the heading is set in the same type as the list entries.

Examples (4) through (6) illustrate how using two differences produces much stronger visual contrast. Example (4) uses a gap and sets the heading in bold type. Example (5) sets the heading in bold type and uses indented bullets to offset the list from the heading. Example (6) increases the size of the heading's font and sets the heading in a different color.

The latter three examples communicate the relationship between the heading and the list entries much more effectively than do the first three examples, and illustrate how size and space can be used to help indicate the relationship between the items.

Positioning

In the English-speaking world, and in other left-to-right languages, we read from left to right and from top to bottom. What is at the top of the page is considered to be more important than what is at the bottom of the page, and, to a lesser extent, things on the left in a row of things are perceived to come first. (In right-to-left languages like Arabic and Hebrew, the right-to-left direction is reversed.)

Thus, the top-left corner of the page is where the eye begins when scanning the page, and so the most important element in the visual hierarchy is usually placed there.

If we have two visual elements A and B, we should ensure that A is positioned either above, or to the left of, element B, when we want to show that:

- Element A is more important than element B; or,

- Element B is a subelement of A; or,

- Element B depends on, logically follows from, or derives from, element A; or,

- Element A is the cause and B is the effect; or

- Element B naturally comes after A in a logical sequence or enumeration.

As an example, let's take one example of poor design that I've encountered recently. One system had a screen for editing customer details that looked roughly like this:

(Retrieve) (Save) (Clear) (Exit)			
Last Name	Smith	First Name	John
Title	Mr.	Date of Birth	1964.03.24
Customer Number	22557788	VIP?	☑
Account Balance	$198.25	Contract Type	Platinum Plan

FIGURE 13-29

Users were expected to enter a value in the *Customer Number* field and then click *Retrieve*. The other fields on the screen would then be populated with the data on file for that particular customer.

The above design is poor because the relationship between the customer number and the remaining fields is not communicated by the visual design.

The data on this screen is dependent on the customer number, because the customer number is the identifying piece of information, or **key**, for a customer record. If the user enters a new customer number and clicks *Retrieve*, the data corresponding to that new customer number will be loaded and presented.

But because the user will start reading the screen from the top left, the user might assume that the last name and first name are identifying the customer record. Additionally, the fact that the user is expected to locate the *Customer Number* field first is troubling; it is buried deep in the screen, and there are no visual cues that it is the most important element upon which the others are dependent. If it is the identifying field upon which the other fields depend, then it should be situated in a place that better communicates its importance: the upper left, where the user begins scanning the screen.

And the fact that the user has to jump from the *Customer Number* field up to the *Retrieve* button is poor design as well. There are no cues that this is how the interaction flow is supposed to work; because we read from left-to-right and from top-to-bottom, jumping from below to above is counterintuitive. The button should be moved so that there is a left-to-right or top-to-bottom flow from the *Customer Number* field to the *Retrieve* button.

Thus, one possibility for an improved layout might be something like the following:

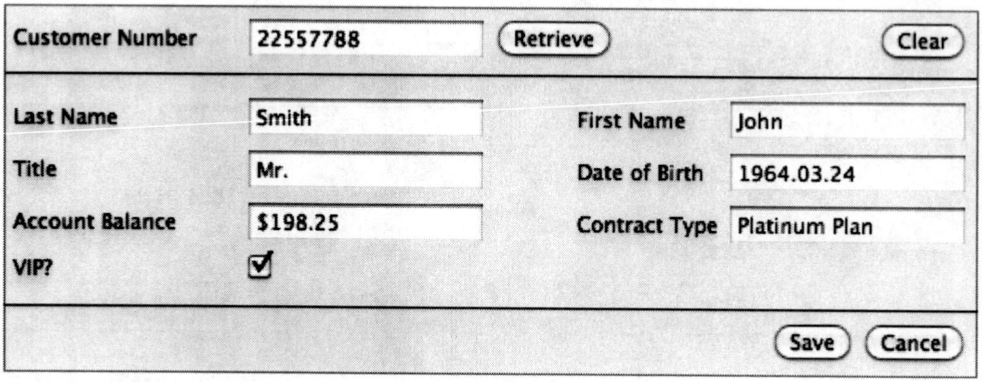

| Customer Number | 22557788 | Retrieve | | | Clear |

Last Name	Smith		First Name	John
Title	Mr.		Date of Birth	1964.03.24
Account Balance	$198.25		Contract Type	Platinum Plan
VIP?	☑			

Save   Cancel

FIGURE 13-30

In this design, it is clearer that the details are dependent upon the chosen customer number. There is a left-to-right flow from the *Customer Number* field to the *Retrieve* button, and there is a top-to-bottom and left-to-right flow that leads towards the finalizing *Save* and *Cancel* buttons.

Practical aspects of visual hierarchy for user interface design

While you may not necessarily explicitly design a visual hierarchy when creating a page composition, an awareness of the general concept of the visual hierarchy and an understanding of how relationships between elements can be expressed can help you produce better designs.

In large project teams, you can try to ensure some degree of visual design consistency throughout your product by creating a style guide that defines the general look-and-feel of the interface in terms of a visual hierarchy. (Style guides will be discussed in Chapter 15.) Writing a style guide is not always easy; it's not always possible to completely document everything that makes up a consistent set of visual designs. But by specifying guidelines or rules for the styles and positioning of headings and other visual elements, and by providing page layout templates and examples, a style guide can help communicate your design intentions to the project team.

Making visual designs look good

Graphic designers often say that aesthetically-pleasing creative works possess **unity**, meaning that everything simply just fits together coherently:

- All the elements on the page appear to belong there;

- There are no unnecessary or extraneous elements; and

- All the elements are arranged in such a way that they appear to belong together.

To achieve unity in your page layouts, keep the following principles in mind:

- **Consistency and continuity**: Visual elements like fonts, colors, rules, icons, and decorations should be used consistently across the composition.

  The same visual style and layout scheme should be repeated across all pages on a website, or across all screens and dialogs in a desktop application, and ideally, this consistency should be maintained across your organization's entire product line.

- **Coherence**: The design should make sense conceptually. Elements should be positioned and styled to reflect their positions in the visual hierarchy of the page. Elements with similar functions and similar importance should be styled with similar attributes (size, color, font, weight); elements that are of the same general type but which differ in importance should share certain attributes but vary others.

  For example, if your design has three levels of headings, they should usually share the same typeface, but the more-important levels of headings should use visual attributes such as a larger type size or a thicker weight to express their relative importance.

- **Simplicity, restraint, and minimalism**: While you do want to make your pages look interesting and eye-catching, this is better achieved with a simple and elegant design rather than one cluttered with unnecessary and excessive decorations and distractions.

- **Balance and dominance**: You want to use the space on the page effectively and attractively. For example, If your page is tightly packed with content on one side, but the other side is empty, your page will look lopsided:

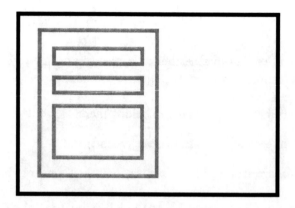

FIGURE 13-31

This page looks like it is going to tip over to one side!

This doesn't necessarily mean that all pages have to be symmetrical, however. Asymmetrical designs tend to look more interesting — graphic designers call this effect **dynamic tension**. Even though an asymmetrical design might have a dominant feature, like a large, eye-catching panel on the left-hand side, the design could still achieve balance by positioning additional elements on the right-hand side:

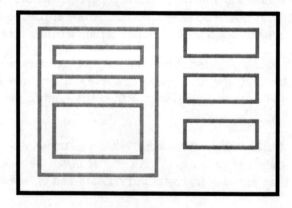

FIGURE 13-32

- **"Good Gestalt"**: You should be able to perceive the design as a coherent whole, rather than a chaotic mish-mash or mosaic of elements.

A design that expresses unity has order and organization to it. You want the viewer to feel that there was an intelligent designer behind the work, and that the designer

170

deliberately and intentionally chose and produced that particular design. The alternative is for the viewer to suspect that the design was slapped together haphazardly or by accident – and you don't want that!

Understanding and redesigning system-supported work

To design a product's interface and interactions effectively, you first need to think about the work that the product will help the user perform.

Work, as we've discussed earlier, is a term that might not be entirely appropriate for all types of software. A user will use a productivity application such as a word processor or a graphics editor to produce a creative work, or some document with business value. Employees of a bank will operate an enterprise system to run the bank's operations and to carry out transactions for customers. For these types of products and systems, work is obviously being done, and this chapter will be very relevant if you're designing and building systems like these.

For many other types of products, and in particular, entertainment and game applications, what the user does with the product can't really be considered "work" in the traditional sense of productivity with some practical or creative end. But even games require skill and effort in order to satisfy some goal, no matter how pointless that goal might be when judged by standards in the real world. For these types of applications, we will still refer to the tasks that the user performs as work, but admittedly, for many of these applications, not all of the material in this chapter will be entirely relevant.

For most productivity applications and enterprise applications, the software helps automate some kind of work that would otherwise have to be done manually. Many enterprise systems projects are introduced as part of an organizational change initiative to improve the efficiency of the organization or to enable the organization to attain a new capacity, such as entering a new market. Often, an enterprise system may be constructed to replace an older application — a **legacy system** — that is no longer cost-effective or meeting the needs of the organization.

In all of these above cases, the new product is an opportunity to do things in a better way than was being done previously. And so, before designing a new product or system, in order to figure out the optimal way to structure the software-supported tasks and actions, it's helpful, and often critically important, to understand the domain and the work. This involves discovering and analyzing how the work is being done currently (whether or not there's already a software solution in place), and what the fundamental essence of the work involves (whether it may be performed with a computer-and-software solution or some other means).

This process of discovery and analysis not only helps the designers understand the context, domain, and work, but can help identify weaknesses and problems that can then be avoided in the new design.

The components of work and workflow

To get work done, individuals engage with tools (either physical tools and devices, or software applications), artifacts (such as paper documents), and people (such as customers and colleagues), in order to achieve some *goal*.

Goals may be chosen by the individual, or, in the context of a workplace, goals will typically be defined by the organization or team. Certain goals will often inherently be part of an individual's job role. So as a first step, understanding the goals of the individual, and the goals of the organization and team, if appropriate, is fundamental to understanding the reason and rationale for why the work is being done in the first place.

Another critical early step in understanding work is to understand the terminology and concepts of the domain, which we've already explored in Chapter 7.

You will also need to understand the characteristics of the users who are performing the work, and the different roles that may be involved in a collaborative activity. We explored understanding user requirements in Chapter 6.

Work involves tasks and actions performed in order to achieve the goals. Decomposing goals into high-level tasks, and then breaking those high-level tasks into subtasks and actions is called a **hierarchical task breakdown**, and is a frequently-used method for analyzing and understanding work.

But work often involves more than just tasks and actions. Rosson and Carroll (2002) argue that work in the context of an organization consists of three dimensions that need to be explored:

- *Activities:* What goals are the individuals or groups pursuing, and what actions do they carry out in pursuing these goals?

- *Artifacts:* What information is retrieved, stored, or created as work is done? What tools or physical artifacts such as paper documents, telephones, e-mail applications, etc., are used to record or communicate information or otherwise facilitate the work?

- *The social context of the workplace:* What roles and responsibilities exist, and what relationships and dependencies exist between individuals and groups? What hierarchical structures and other formal or informal groupings exist in the organization?

Another important concept, whenever work involves multiple people, is that of **workflow**, i.e., how individuals collaborate in order to complete a complex activity or **business process**. As a simple example, in a game of chess, there are two players, and they take turns making moves.

A description of a workflow defines:

- what subtasks of the activity or task exist;

- who (individuals, roles, or groups) is responsible for performing each subtask;

- what inputs and output artifacts or deliverables exist for each subtask;

- what stages or states the artifacts may have, and the conditions under which these stages or states change;

- how and when subtasks and the overall activity are deemed to be complete; and,

- how information and artifacts are passed between individuals or groups.

Additionally, a workflow description could include the event or events that trigger the initiation of the business process.

As an example of a workflow scenario, let's take the hypothetical case of an organization that administers a pension plan.

175

When a member of the pension plan applies for retirement, the request (which may take the form of a telephone call, a letter, or a filled-out application form) will first be received by a customer service representative. The representative will enter the data into the computer system, and if all of the required data is present, the system will calculate an estimate of the benefits. Once this has been done, a manager is notified, and the manager must inspect the calculation results. When the manager gives approval, the customer service representative is notified, and then the representative prints out a hardcopy of the benefits statement and a form for the customer to sign. The representative then places these documents in an envelope and places the envelope in an outbox. The contents of the outbox are routinely collected and taken to the mailroom, where appropriate postage is applied, and the envelope is sent into the postal system. Once the member has signed and returned the documents, then the customer service representative enters the confirmation into the system. The system updates the member's status to *retiree* and regularly-scheduled benefit payments begin.

Workflows and business processes can be simple sequential series of steps, but more often they will include decisions or judgements to be made, which can lead to different branches of steps, or series of steps (i.e., loops) that are repeated until some condition is satisfied.

Organizations may also have business rules that staff are to follow in order to guarantee standards of service, quality, or safety. For example, if the quantity on hand of an inventory item ever falls below a specific threshold, then an order shall be placed to an appropriate supplier to replenish the items.

Note, of course, that different organizations have different levels of formality, and so business processes and business rules may not necessarily be formally written down in documents, and if they are, the real processes that are actually being followed may not match the officially documented processes!

To document and communicate workflows, business processes, and task flows, you can write free-form textual descriptions, employ *use case* templates, or draw diagrams such as flowcharts. We will introduce and discuss these techniques in Chapter 15.

Workflow vs. task flow

We should note that the term *workflow* is sometimes also used to refer to how an individual performs a task with a software application.

In this book, we'll use *workflow* to refer to the interactions and the structured processes that groups of people follow in order to collaboratively get work done in an organization, and we'll use the terminology **task flow** to describe the steps, actions, and decisions that an individual uses to perform a specific task. A task flow may be a part of a workflow.

Techniques for investigating how work is currently done

To find out how work is currently being done, you can perform **ethnographic research** — in other words, analyzing the activities, artifacts, environment, and culture of the work and the workplace. By definition, this can't be done sitting in your office; you need to be physically present with the people who are doing the work, at the place where they do the work.

To do this research, consider techniques such as the following:

- Interview the people who are actually getting the work done, as well as their managers and supervisors.

- Consider performing **user observation** or **job shadowing**, where you sit down with users and watch them go about their daily tasks. If you observe any difficulties, cases where workarounds are needed, or situations where official processes are not being followed, record your observations and ask about them. These may be opportunities for designing better processes.

- Observe the physical workplace. Keep an eye out for aids and crutches like cheat-sheets, or reminders written on sticky notes. These are often clues that users find an existing system difficult to use.

- Identify artifacts and tools. Determine how artifacts such as documents are passed between individuals or groups, and draw diagrams to record and help facilitate discussion of this knowledge.

- Identify the people, such as customers, whom the workers interact with in the course of performing their duties. If appropriate, speak with them.

- If you are working on a project to replace a legacy system, inspect any specifications or other documentation created during the design and construction of that system. This type of investigation is sometimes referred to as **documentation archaeology**. Recognize, however, that the documentation may be inaccurate or out-of-date. Official procedures may not be being followed, because users find them incomplete, too abstract, inappropriate, or incorrect.

To document and communicate workflows, business processes, and task flows, you can write free-form descriptions or draw flowchart diagrams, or you may wish to use some of the specification techniques that we will introduce in Chapter 15.

Work redesign and business process reengineering

When new enterprise software systems are introduced in an organization, it is usually because the system is intended to increase the efficiency of administering some area of the business (leading to a long-term cost savings), or because some organizational problem or market opportunity has been recognized, and the software is intended to solve (or help solve) the problem or facilitate the exploitation of the opportunity. The software will typically facilitate business processes and enforce rules, or it will facilitate operations in a way that results in less inefficiency and waste.

In many cases, the rollout of new enterprise software introduces new business processes and other changes to the way work is done. This may involve fundamental changes to individual workers' responsibilities and task flows. Introducing these changes often requires **change management** efforts such as (1) communicating the reasons for the new processes, (2) training programs, (3) coaching, and (4) periodic review and process adjustment.

As a software designer or business analyst, you may be in a position of being given a set of new or redesigned business processes, and your task is to design the application to match them. Or, you may hold responsibility for analyzing the organization's domain and problems and designing the new business processes, and then introducing these business processes into the business through the design and deployment of the software.

To redesign work and business processes (**business process reengineering**), you can use your understanding of how the work is currently being done and what the current problems are, and use this as the basis for designing improvements that improve the situation. When possible, you should generate alternatives, encourage discussion and review of the alternatives, and then compare and evaluate the alternatives to choose the best solutions.

Redesigned business processes and task flows may bring about increased effectiveness by achieving one or more of the following:

- Faster work;

- Fewer errors and oversights (such as lost or forgotten files or cases);

- Faster response time;

- Higher throughput;

- Higher quality (for example, by means of more quality checks and controls);

- Less waste and inefficiency;

- More management oversight, such as better status reporting, or more measurability of progress and quality;

- Improved ease-of-use, reduced frustration, and higher job satisfaction for users.

Deciding what functions the application will provide

As a part of determining and deciding what work activities and artifacts your product or system will be concerned with, you will need to define more specifically the features and functionality it will have. By doing this, you will be defining the product or system's **scope**.

In most projects, it is important to get a first definition of the scope early on so that estimates of effort can be generated, an initial budget can be set, and the appropriate resources can begin to be acquired. The scope will typically change after this first definition, but **scope creep** — the gradual and continual addition of desired features and functionality to the scope of a project — if not managed and controlled, can easily cause a project to exceed budget and deadline constraints.

In a project where the list of desired features and functionality is frequently changing or growing, the use of an agile methodology, in which a backlog of features and requirements is maintained, and in which the prioritization and scheduling is reviewed and adjusted at regular intervals, can be a more effective way of managing changes and additions to the scope of a project.

Choosing the features and functionality can be trickier than it initially sounds. There are often many possible alternatives to consider and choose from, and different stakeholders will have different opinions on what functionality is considered critical. It often becomes a highly political affair.

For many tasks and features, you will often need to decide what parts of the task the user will be responsible for performing, and what the system will be responsible for. How much of the work will the system automate? How much data or ongoing control will the user have to provide to enable the system to do its task appropriately? How many details will the user need to know and memorize, and how much will the application be able to internalize or abstract away? And how much control over the details of the task will the user have? Expert users will often expect more control, but this increased complexity will confuse new and intermediate users.

In Chapter 15, we will continue exploring these questions and themes. We'll take a look at techniques for documenting workflows and task flows. We'll also begin to explore the design of the interfaces and interactions for the scope of functionality you've identified for your product, and we'll cover a number of techniques for specifying those designs.

15

Designing and specifying user interfaces and interactions

Let's now take a look at the process of designing and specifying the user interface and interactions for a software application.

The process of *designing* something is difficult to separate from the process of *recording* the design. While you may have ideas for the design of a product in your head, these ideas don't become an actual design until you begin making them concrete by putting them down on paper or in electronic form.

Designs need not necessarily be perfectly structured and complete. If you're designing a small product that you'll be building yourself, and you have a general idea of how it will work, then just sketching out a few rough ideas for screen layouts on paper can often be quite sufficient for your needs.

But most software is developed by teams within organizations, and the software is typically either being built to serve the needs of a specific client, or it is being developed as a product for sale to a particular market segment. In this environment, you may be a designer or analyst who needs to communicate the intended design to the team members who will build and test the product. You'll need to explain and justify your designs to the client or the marketing department and senior management in order to gain approval. And in order to effectively estimate and plan the project, the team needs to know what is going to be built.

The traditional way of recording and communicating the intended design of a software system is to write a **specification**.

Formal specifications are often criticized by advocates of agile approaches, and it is true that formal specifications are not appropriate in all project situations. It is also true that many specifications are simply incompetently written and are entirely ineffective for their intended purpose. Nevertheless, writing a specification often still has value in many common software development project scenarios. In particular:

• Writing down a concrete design before implementation begins will force you to discover, think through, and resolve problems and issues earlier rather than later. It is vastly easier and much more cost-effective to correct a document in the early stage of a project than it is to rework and retest software that has already been built and delivered.

• A specification document serves as a tangible artifact that collects, records, and makes sense of the team's knowledge, design decisions, and design rationale. A specification document is something tangible that can be reviewed and discussed.

• A specification serves as a communication medium between designers, developers, testers, and project managers. Developers will build the product according to the specification. Testers will use the specification to check the correctness of the implementation of the product (does the product actually function as described in the specification?). And the specification enables detailed work breakdown, estimation, and resource planning for the implementation and testing phases of the project.

Specifications are an appropriate and suitable approach in many project situations. If specifications are used in a project that is structured according to the textbook waterfall model, however, there usually exists the fundamental assumption that it is possible to fully understand the requirements and then produce a coherent and complete design before implementation begins. That assumption is particularly problematic in those cases where you may be designing and building systems for clients who doesn't really know what they want, or where you are building a product for a product-market segment that is constantly changing due to competitive pressures, rapid technological change, or other external factors.

In contrast, agile approaches prioritize the creation of working software over the creation of extensive "heavyweight" documentation. This does not mean that no documentation whatsoever will be generated, but the cost of producing any document must be weighed against the value that the document will provide, and typically, a "just enough, and just good enough" mentality pervades over an insistence on having a perfect and complete set of documents.

Agile approaches and specifications are certainly not incompatible: In an agile environment, a rudimentary, "bare-bones" outline of specification could be gradually created and then iteratively and incrementally improved upon and revised throughout the project. Alternatively, some agile projects may prefer to use techniques such as informal user stories and prototypes to generate and reason about ideas and initial design solutions, and to communicate the chosen designs. Then, as iterative review and reworking of the actual working software takes place, each iteration will lead to an incrementally better and more complete version of the product.

What methods are appropriate for your project will depend on what type of product you are building and what skills your team possesses. In this chapter, we'll take a look at a wide range of both formal and informal techniques. By being aware of the options, you can make informed choices.

First, though, let's examine the formal approach of writing a specification.

What is a specification?

Given a set of requirements, there may be many different possible designs for a software product or system that will satisfy those requirements. A **specification** is a detailed description of one specific, concrete design solution for a software product or system that will meet the requirements of the client or customer and other stakeholders.

As the name implies, the essence of a specification is that it should be *specific*. A description of a software system that is full of ambiguities cannot really be considered to be a specification.

Ideally, you should be able to hand a specification to a development team, and the developers should then be able to build the software as described, with a minimum of questions and clarifications needed. In reality, it is virtually impossible to create a specification for a non-trivial product that is complete and flawless to a degree that necessitates no clarification, but it is the ideal, if unattainable, state that should be kept in mind.

Types of specifications

The design of a complex software application is frequently divided into two separate but interrelated specifications:

- A **functional specification** describes what features and functionality the product will have. It describes, from the user's point of view, the appearance and behavior of the application's user interface: how the features and functions will appear, and how the user will interact with and operate them.

- Given a functional specification, there may be many different ways to implement that design in software. A **technical specification** describes how the functionality will be constructed in terms of components such as components, schemas, modules, classes, algorithms, and technical interfaces (such as data exchange file formats and protocols).

In this book, being that we are concerned with the design (but not the technical implementation details) of the user interface and user experience for software applications, we will concentrate primarily on functional specifications.

From abstract to precise

In an idealized waterfall process, requirements are first discovered and documented. Using the requirements as the basis, a functional specification is created. Then, given the functional specification, a technical specification is created to set out the details of how the product will be constructed to fulfill the functional specification. Implementation of the software then follows from the functional and technical specifications. Given the implemented product, testers can then verify that the product matches the functional specification.

This sequence of documentation artifacts facilitates moving from high-level project and product goals, to requirements, to a specific user-facing design, to a specific technical implementation design, to the actual implementation.

The use of separate artifacts (requirements, functional, and technical specifications) also facilitates the assignment of work to those staff members who have the appropriate knowledge for each task: domain experts or business analysts might typically write the requirements and functional specifications, while technical architects and developers typically create the technical specifications. There can be many variations on this, of course. Sometimes a single specification that combines functional and technical aspects might be suitable, for instance, and such a specification could be written by a single person who possesses skills in all of the appropriate areas.

As we've discussed earlier in this chapter and throughout this book, however, the "textbook" waterfall approach is a convenient and simple conceptual model, but is rarely workable in real-life projects. Most projects that intend to follow the waterfall model usually devolve into a continuous, ongoing state of correcting and revising documents and implementation artifacts as problems, issues, and requirements changes are detected during implementation, testing, and deployment. But this type of ongoing change can be managed using the tools of iteration and incrementalism.

Adding agility to the specification process: Iteration and incrementalism

In actual practice, and whether it is intentionally planned or not, software specification generally happens in iterations. If specifications and implementation artifacts are going to undergo constant change and correction, then rather than have these occurring haphazardly, it is a good practice to embrace the inevitable change by intentionally structuring the project to use iterations. In each iteration, the design and implementation of the product or system incrementally take shape, becoming more complete and more refined. Over multiple iterations, the product should gradually approach the "ideal" solution (though it may never reach the "ideal" state, as requirements tend to change throughout the life of a project).

Whether a formal specification or more informal techniques are employed, an incremental and iterative approach to design and specification will typically take the following form:

- In the earliest iterations, as various possible designs are being discovered and investigated, high-level, general descriptions will be generated and recorded. These descriptions are rough sketches of the solution at an abstract level: Screen mockups will be low-fidelity wireframes, and the descriptions will be incomplete, with many ambiguities and gaps and questions that will need to be resolved. This allows multiple alternatives to be explored, evaluated, and revised with little risk and without a large investment.

- As more information is gathered, as decisions are made, and as problems and questions are worked out and resolved, the descriptions will be revised and refined to become more complete and precise. Details will be fleshed out at increasingly finer levels of abstraction. If the goal is to produce a formal specification, the descriptions will gradually reach the state of being an complete and coherent specification for the purposes of implementation. If the goal is to produce a high-fidelity prototype, the prototype will increasingly approach the state of being an accurate representation of the desired design of the product.

Criteria to consider when choosing the appropriate design and specification approach

When deciding whether formal or informal design and specification techniques are right for your project, you may wish to consider the following factors:

- *Team size:* The larger the team, the more it becomes necessary to introduce formal processes and documentation, to minimize duplicated and wasted effort, and to prevent miscommunication and misunderstanding.

- *Skills of team members:* Small, agile teams typically work best with a highly-skilled, experienced team of generalists. In larger projects and projects dealing with complicated domains, it is usually the more senior and specialized staff members who design the product and write the specifications; more junior staff then use that knowledge and information to build and test the product.

- *Interpersonal dynamics:* A team consisting of people who get along with each other is more likely to succeed using agile processes and informal techniques. Teams with more complicated dynamics and politics might intentionally use stricter processes as a means of demarcating responsibilities and managing conflicts.

- *Product and domain complexity:* Complex products dealing with complex domains will require more formality and structure when specifying rules and behavior.

- *Risk, compliance, and regulatory issues:* Products and systems that deal with safety-critical or highly-regulated domains such as finance, medicine, or aviation, can be subject to strict regulatory requirements, and may be subject to certification processes, inspections, or audits. Some firms also adhere to quality management systems such as ISO 9000. In such cases, formal specifications and project plans may be a necessity for providing evidence of sufficient diligence and process control.

- *Technical risk:* Some products that include groundbreaking or unproven technology might in some cases benefit from the preliminary research and planning that the development of a specification involves. In other cases, however, lightweight, iterative cycles of experimentation, investigation, and refinement may be more suitable for novel products and technologies.

Specification techniques

Let's now examine a number of techniques that can be used for designing and specifying the user-facing functionality of software. You will typically choose a combination of techniques as appropriate for the characteristics of your product and the degree of formality of your project.

The techniques that follow have been arranged into two categories: those that are primarily useful for defining product *appearance*, and those that are primarily useful for defining product *behavior*. Note, however, that some techniques involve a little bit of both.

Techniques for defining product appearance

High-fidelity mockups and prototypes

A screen **mockup** is an illustration of what some "place" in the application — a screen, a window, a dialog, or a page — will look like. A **high-fidelity mockup** is an illustration that is intended to realistically approximate the intended appearance of the user interface (in contrast to a *low-fidelity mockup*, which is intentionally created as a "rough sketch" that does not look like a real working product).

A high-fidelity mockup is usually a static image, with no interactivity.

Figure 15-1 is an example of a high-fidelity mockup, which was constructed with HTML, CSS, and several simple images:

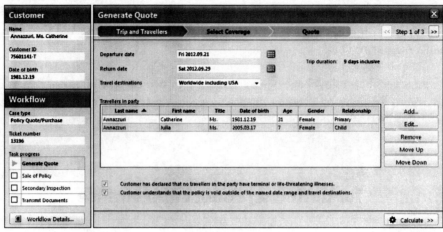

FIGURE 15-1

As static mockups do not specify behavior, additional specification techniques should be used in conjunction with mockups to specify what will happen when each control is activated by the user.

Alternatively, to demonstrate the product's intended behavior, a **high-fidelity prototype** can be constructed. In contrast to a mockup, a prototype is an interactive piece of software. However, a prototype is not a full-fledged, fully-functional product. It is a *simulation* of a working product, or some limited parts of a working product. Typically, a prototype will only be able to demonstrate a handful of very limited scenarios or features.

There is usually some coding involved in constructing a prototype, but this code will be a produced in a quick-and-dirty fashion, with the intention of achieving results quickly. The code produced will be only enough to simulate the display of the results of some action within some specific scenario. That means that a prototype will usually not have a database or any actual business logic implemented in it.

Additionally, prototypes are very often built using simpler technologies than what the final product will actually be constructed with. For instance, a database-driven Java/J2EE web application might initially be simulated up using a prototype that consists only of a series of static HTML pages. The HTML pages will show controls such as buttons, and clicking on a control will simply have the effect of navigating to another HTML page that shows the simulated effects of the action. (Such a prototype is essentially a series of interlinked static mockups.)

Imagine a rudimentary mockup of a web-based mortgage calculator. The initial page may be a static HTML page with a form in which various input data values have been pre-populated. Clicking on the "Calculate" button on that page would then simply transfer the user to a calculation results page, itself another static page, which shows the simulated results of the calculation. Modifying the data on the initial page would not actually influence the data displayed on the results page because those displayed results are all completely fake (but plausible enough to let viewers understand how the application will work).

Prototypes are usually built to demonstrate some aspect of the product, and so they are typically limited either in *breadth* or *depth* of functionality. If a prototype is limited in *breadth*, it will only support a handful of the features intended for the actual product, but it will demonstrate those selected features in detail. If a prototype is limited in *depth*, it will include many features, but will not demonstrate those features in great detail.

High-fidelity mockups and prototypes are useful for demonstrating and discussing design ideas with clients and other stakeholders. Unfortunately, because the mockups and prototypes can look like real working software, stakeholders who see them sometimes get the impression that the product or system has already been built and is working, leading to misunderstandings about development and delivery schedules.

Another risk of prototypes is that if they actually do the work of the product (i.e., the behavior is not entirely faked), management will be tempted to use the prototype as the actual deliverable product itself, despite the fact that the prototype was hastily constructed without the proper technical architecture and planning needed to support long-term maintenance. Extending and maintaining a poorly-written code base can be extraordinarily costly and tends to cause serious product quality issues.

For the purpose of aiding and guiding implementation efforts, high-fidelity mockups and prototypes are useful in that they give developers a very concrete visual depiction of the intended appearance of a product, so there is a better chance that what the developers implement will actually match that intended appearance. A disadvantage, though, is that high-fidelity prototypes can be very time-consuming to build.

Low-fidelity mockups, which we will explore next, can avoid some of the problems we've discussed.

Low-fidelity (wireframe) mockups and prototypes

A **low-fidelity mockup**, as was mentioned briefly earlier, is an illustration of some part of a user interface, executed as an informal "rough sketch". Low-fidelity mockups are also frequently referred to as **wireframes**.

A low-fidelity mockup intentionally does not attempt to look like the pixel-perfect final appearance; instead, it represents controls and other visual elements using simple outlines, and focuses on showing only the basic layout of the visual elements.

A low-fidelity mockup can be drawn on paper, or constructed with wireframing or diagramming software. The following is an example of a mockup drawn using the popular *Balsamiq Mockups* tool:

FIGURE 15-2

Because low-fidelity mockups are rough sketches, they are much easier to modify, and this supports rapid iteration and exploration of design ideas. Customers and stakeholders who see low-fidelity mockups will also be able to recognize that the mockups are only images, and not real working software.

An interactive, low-fidelity prototype can be constructed by using wireframing software that allows you to make controls clickable. Clicking on a control triggers navigation to a different mockup image. In this way, simple interaction scenarios can be simulated.

Designers can hand low-fidelity mockups and prototypes to developers, and it should usually be sufficient information for the developers to use to construct the implementation of the layout of the user interface. However, to ensure that the appearance of the controls, colors, fonts, and layouts is correct and consistent, a *style guide* (discussed next) is recommended for use in conjunction with low-fidelity mockups.

Style guides

A **style guide** is a document that defines the general rules for the graphic design of an application's visual appearance. It describes the structure of the general page layout, indicates the color scheme and rules for applying the colors, and precisely defines the appearance of visual elements such as headlines, text, and user interface controls. Developers can then use these guidelines in conjunction with low-fidelity mockups to ensure that implemented user interfaces match the intended visual appearance.

Style guides for user interfaces could also include some limited descriptions of behavior, such as what kind of animated effect should appear when a button is pressed and released. The style guide is also a good place to describe common or repeating elements or controls. For example, a style guide for a website will often define what elements and controls will appear in the website's header and footer (which appear on every page).

While there is no standard format or template for creating a style guide, it should be kept as simple as possible. One general approach is to list each class of element, such as Heading 1, Heading 2, Heading 3, Button, etc., and specify attributes such as font typeface, font size, color, spacing, and so on for each. Of course, by doing this, it is possible to have conflicting rules, and there will always be the potential for multiple interpretations of combinations of rules. So, like all other design artifacts, expect revisions to the style guide throughout the project.

Navigation maps

For applications and websites that feature multiple "places" that can be visited, creating a **navigation map** diagram that depicts the paths by which the various places can be reached can be a useful specification tool.

Chapter 12 discussed the process of designing navigation maps as part of formulating an application's interaction concept.

Techniques for defining product behavior

User stories

User stories, which we encountered and discussed in Chapter 6, are short descriptions of features or functions of the product, ideally with a mention of the rationale for a user would need that function. User stories should be brief enough to be written on an index card.

An example of a user story is:

> *As a frequent flier cardholder, I want to check my points balance online so that I can determine whether I am eligible for any rewards.*

User stories are an informal way of exploring and negotiating what behavioral requirements will form the scope of a new product. In agile methodologies such as Scrum, user stories are then used as items of work for planning, estimating, and scheduling the implementation of the product.

User stories are good as a lightweight requirements management technique, but they are less suitable as a specification technique for precisely defining finer details of the desired product behavior. While relatively simple products might be sufficiently describable (for the purposes of implementation) with a set of user story cards, if your product will involve complex rules and interaction behaviors, you will probably need to supplement story cards with additional techniques to capture and communicate the appropriate information.

Use cases

A **use case** is a textual description of an interaction for some particular way that users are expected to use the application to achieve some goal. The interaction is broken down into a sequence of steps, which may be actions performed by a user, the system, or other *actors*. (Actors could be other human users in various roles, other computer systems, or entities such as organizations.)

An e-commerce website might have use cases with titles such as "Add item to shopping cart", "Checkout", "Check status of order", and "Create a new user account".

A use case explains the sequence of steps for a **standard scenario,** but typically includes alternative paths to handle cases such as errors. In addition to the sequences of steps for the standard scenario and alternate scenario, it is common to include further relevant information related to the use case, and so you will want to find or create a template for writing use cases so that all of the use cases in your project follow a consistent format. Figure 15-3 shows an example of a use case structured according to a basic template:

Use case ID	UC001
Title	Make a donation
Goal	User makes a donation to a project
Primary actor	User (website visitor)
Preconditions	At least one project has been set up in the system
Assumptions	User possesses a credit card
Trigger condition	User decides that he or she would like to make a donation to a project
Main success scenario	1. User selects the *Make a donation* option 2. System presents a donation form page 3. User selects a project to donate to 4. User enters a donation amount 5. User selects a currency 6. Optionally, user enters a message 7. User enters name and address details 8. User enters credit card payment details 9. User submits information 10. System presents summary page of information for review 11. User reviews information 12. User confirms the information and agrees to proceed with the donation 13. System processes the payment 14. System provides confirmation of payment and donation 15. Optionally, user prints copy of receipt
Alternative scenarios (extensions)	12a. User chooses to revise the information. System returns to the donation form page (step 2) and pre-populates the form with the previously-entered information 12b. User cancels the transaction 14a. System reports a transaction processing failure (e.g., invalid credit card number)

FIGURE 15-3

The "Alternative scenarios (extensions)" section lists alternative events that can occur at each step in the main success scenario. For instance, at step 12, rather than proceeding with the donation, one of the events described in steps 12a or 12b could occur instead.

Alternative scenarios could involve substeps, in which case you might number them using a scheme such as 12a(1), 12a(2), and so on.

One could also add many additional fields to this basic use case template. Project management metadata such as Priority, Creation Date, Target Delivery Date, and so on, are common in many projects. Use cases that adhere to a very detailed template are sometimes referred to as **fully-dressed use cases**, whereas **casual use cases** adhere to more minimalistic templates.

Use cases can describe system behavior at multiple levels of abstraction. Alistair Cockburn's book *Writing Effective Use Cases* (Cockburn, 2000) categorizes use cases into several levels:

- A **high-level** or **summary use case**, also known as a **cloud-level use case**, describes in broad terms how the system will support some high-level goal. Steps are stated in general terms without mentioning any specific details of the user interface. High-level use cases can often include references to lower-level use cases.

  High-level use cases help explain the context of the system and can be used to detail the lifecycle processes involved in large goals. For example, a high-level use case might be "Prepare accounting year-end", and it would reference the lower-level use cases that users would use to complete that work.

- A **user-goal level use case**, or **sea-level use case**, is the level most useful for designing interactions. User-goal level use cases correspond to tasks that the user will want to perform in order to achieve a goal. Examples of such use cases would be "Record an invoice", "Pay a bill", or "Generate a trial balance".

- **Subfunction-level use cases**, or **underwater use cases**, correspond to fine-grained tasks that users or the system must perform, but which are supporting functions that themselves do not directly make any progress towards achieving a business goal (but nonetheless are still necessary due to the nature or design of the solution). Examples are "Log in to the system" or "Save the document to disk". User-goal level use cases will often include references to subfunction-level use cases.

When describing the steps of the interactions, the level of detail you employ can vary depending on what you wish to achieve. For instance, one could write "The user prints a copy of the receipt", which is abstract: it indicates the user's intention, and does not mention which keys must be pressed or what on-screen controls must be clicked or touched.

Alternatively, you could very specifically refer to the controls, leading to a series of steps such as: "The user clicks the *View Receipt* button. The system displays the receipt. The user clicks the *Print* button or presses Ctrl+P. The *Print* dialog appears. The user adjusts options if necessary and clicks *OK* or presses Enter."

The former style, using abstract descriptions, is especially appropriate when you are exploring and discussing general design options. The high level of abstraction intentionally leaves the specific design open for later decision.

The latter style, with specific references to user-interface controls, could be useful if you are fleshing out and finalizing a particular design. However, it can also be argued that specific references to user interface controls do not belong in use cases. While being very specific can make the steps clearer to understand, it also has some disadvantages:

- First, it can obscure the user's *intentions* — what the user is really trying to accomplish at each step — which is largely what you are trying to capture in a use case. For example, if you write, "The user presses the F5 key", it may not be clear what the user actually intends to accomplish here. Perhaps F5 is the shortcut key assigned to the "refresh" function, in which case you could instead write, "The user refreshes the display by pressing the F5 key". But it is difficult to be consistent about writing this way, especially when a team is doing the writing, and such descriptions can get out of hand if there are multiple ways of activating a function: "The user refreshes the display by pressing the F5 key, by clicking on the *Refresh* button in the toolbar, or by choosing *View | Refresh* in the pull-down menu".

- Second, if you write your use cases using references to specific controls too prematurely in the design process, you may find that you are making assumptions and decisions that limit your thinking about what solutions are possible. You can begin to artificially restrict the design choices you actually have.

- Third, if at some later point you decide to change the controls or keystrokes, so that, for instance, F10 becomes the refresh keystroke instead of F5, then updating all of the references in all of the use cases becomes an arduous and error-prone task.

A general solution that seems to work reasonably well in practice is this: Use relatively abstract descriptions in use cases, and then supplement the use cases with screen mockups, which show the appearance of the places in the application, together with *behavior tables* (discussed later in this section), which give specific details of what controls and keystroke commands exist and what behavior they will produce when activated. Additional explanatory annotations can be added to these artifacts, or in general specifications documents, if any of the mappings between the abstract action descriptions in the use cases and the actual user interface controls are unclear.

Scenarios

A use case is intended to be a description of an interaction or process that may contain

196

loops and alternate paths. Let's define a **scenario** as one specific *path* through a use case, with specific mention of the options chosen by the user and the data that is entered or presented.

Just as we discussed for use cases, the level of abstraction used in a scenario can vary depending on your needs.

Here is an example of a scenario that is a path through the "Make a donation" use case presented earlier in Figure 15-3. You'll notice that the level of abstraction in this example has been made more specific than in the use case; we're naming the specific buttons and controls that the user is interacting with.

1. User clicks the *Make a donation* button.

2. System presents a donation form page.

3. The user selects "Earthquake reconstruction" as the project to donate to.

4. User enters "100.00" a donation amount.

5. User selects "US Dollars" as the currency.

6. User leaves the message area blank.

7. User enters her name as "Jane Doe" and enters her address as "123 Main Street, Anytown WA, 12345".

8. User enters a valid credit card number, expiry date, and security code.

9. User submits the information by clicking the *Submit* button.

10. System presents a summary page of information for review.

11. User reviews information.

12. User confirms the information and agrees to proceed with the donation by clicking the *Donate* button.

13. System processes the payment.

14. System provides confirmation of payment and donation.

15. User clicks the *Print Receipt* button to print a copy of the receipt.

Scenarios are often most useful when used in conjunction with other techniques. For example, screen mockups and prototypes can show what the product will look like, but the features and interactions that the product will support are not always immediately evident from looking at mockups or examining a prototype. Scenarios can be an effective way of providing **walkthroughs** or **tours** through screen mockups and prototypes, to explain what features are available and how to use them.

Interaction sequence tables

An **interaction sequence table** describes the steps of an interaction scenario, again in sequential narrative form, but it presents the information in a tabular format that more clearly delineates the separation of responsibilities between the user and the system. It can help make the connection between actions (stimuli) and responses more explicit. As an example, here is the previous "Make a donation" scenario again, reworked into an interaction sequence table:

User action	System response
Selects the *Make a donation* button	Presents a donation form page
Selects "Earthquake reconstruction" as the project to donate to	-
Enters "100.00" as the donation amount	-
Selects "US Dollars" as the currency	-
Leaves message area blank	-
Enters her name as "Jane Doe" and enters her address as "123 Main Street, Anytown WA, 12345"	-
Enters a valid credit card number, expiry date, and security code	-
Submits the information by clicking the *Submit* button	Presents a summary page of information for review
Reviews and confirms the information by clicking the *Donate* button	Processes payment and provides confirmation of payment and donation
Clicks the *Print Receipt* button	Prints a copy of the receipt

FIGURE 15-4

Test cases

A **test case** is a scenario that is written specifically for use in verifying that the product actually functions as designed. A test case traditionally consists of a sequential set of

198

steps presented in a tabular format, much like in an interaction sequence table. Each step first describes a specific action to be carried out, and then states the expected results (if any) of that action.

Test cases may be executed manually by a tester, or, the execution of test cases can be automated. Automating test cases will reduce labor in the long run, but the initial investment of automating tests can be very costly, and there is a maintenance cost involved, because automated test cases will need to be revised whenever the relevant product functionality and behavior changes.

When executing a test case, each step is performed in sequence, and the product's response is compared with the expected result for each step. If the product's response matches the expected response for all steps, then the test case has passed for that execution. If any expected result does not match, then the test case has failed for that execution. Throughout a project, test cases will be repeatedly executed against different versions of the software, so a test case that fails when tested with one iteration of the software may pass when tested with another version.

Our example "Make a donation" scenario could be turned into a test case such as the following:

Step	User action	Expected response	OK/ NOK
1	Select the *Make a donation* button	System presents a donation form page	
2	Select "Earthquake reconstruction" as the project to donate to	-	
3	Enter "100.00" as the donation amount	-	
4	Select "US Dollars" as the currency	-	
5	Leave message area blank	-	
6	Enter name as "Jane Doe" and enter address as "123 Main Street, Anytown WA, 12345"	-	
7	Enter a valid credit card number, expiry date, and security code	-	

Step	User action	Expected response	OK/ NOK
8	Submit the information by clicking the *Submit* button	System presents a summary page showing all of the information entered, with the exception of the credit card number, which should be obscured	
9	Review and confirm the information by clicking the *Donate* button	System provides confirmation of payment and donation; today's date, name "Jane Doe", donation amount US $100.00, and project "Earthquake reconstruction" are clearly shown	
10	Click the *Print Receipt* button	System prints a copy of the receipt with today's date, name "Jane Doe", donation amount US $100.00, and project "Earthquake reconstruction" clearly shown	

FIGURE 15-5

In theory, the "OK/NOK" column would be filled out, usually electronically in a test case management system, each time the test case is executed. If the system's response matches the expected response, then "OK" would be recorded in that column. In case of a mismatch, a "NOK" (meaning "Not OK") would be recorded and the test case execution would be considered to have failed.

Test cases often need to be accompanied with appropriate supporting test data. For example, a financial application may need interest rate tables or customer history data to be loaded into the database before calculations can take place. There may be other prerequisite conditions that are expected to be in place before a particular test case is executed, and such conditions should be documented either within or alongside the test case.

In the agile community, a large set of automated test cases is often considered to be a superior substitute for a formal specification for the purpose of defining the product's behavior. Strictly speaking, test cases are not a true form of specification, because a test case only describes the correct behavior of the system under one particular set of inputs, whereas an ideal and properly-written specification would specify the correct behavior for all possible circumstances. However, for many project, a large (and continuously evolving) set of test cases can certainly suffice to define and enforce the intended product behavior for the most common scenarios.

Flowcharts

Flowcharts are boxes-and-arrows diagrams that can be used to depict processes or algorithms that contain sequential steps, repetitive sequences of steps (i.e., loops), and decision points with alternative paths. In the context of user interface design, flowcharts are useful for describing workflows, task flows, and rules in an application.

Flowcharts are popular because they are easy to construct, and the graphical nature of the diagrams makes them more visually appealing and more accessible to non-specialists than lengthy textual descriptions.

Here is a simple example of a flowchart representing the task flow for a simple scenario:

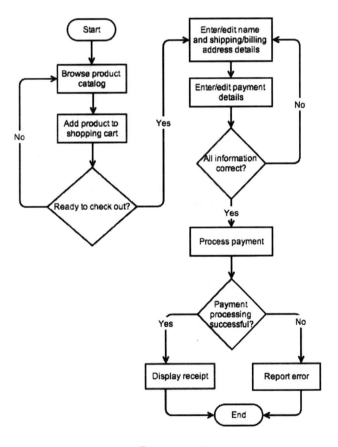

FIGURE 15-6

Although there are many variations of flowchart notations, the traditional basic flow-chart diagram has start and end points, rectangular boxes representing actions or states, and arrows denoting the acceptable paths of control flow. Diamond shapes represent decision points with multiple outgoing arrows; the choice of arrow to follow depends on some condition described within the diamond shape.

Not all application scenarios can be easily captured in a flowchart. For example, event-driven behavior, complex logic with conditions depending on multiple states or variables, the manipulation of complex data structures, and concurrent behavior can often be difficult to depict using a flowchart. Large flowchart diagrams with overlapping and crossing paths can also become unwieldy to construct and interpret.

UML 2.0 activity diagrams

The Unified Modelling Language (UML) 2.0 standard includes **activity diagrams** as one of the standard diagram types. UML activity diagrams can be seen as a next-generation flowcharting technique, with notational conveniences for representing concurrent activities, the synchronization of activities performed by multiple actors, nested flows, guard conditions (conditions that must be true for a transition to take place), and so on.

Figure 15-7 gives an example of an activity diagram. Two elements that may require explanation are the following:

- The black bars indicate the beginning and end of a set of tasks that will be performed in parallel. So in this example, the payment processing and the display of the progress indicator occur concurrently. When both tasks have completed (in this case, the processing of the payment is the key "blocker" task), the execution flows from the concurrent tasks are "joined" and execution continues from the bottom black bar.

- The arrow leading from the topmost *Start* symbol leads to the upper inset box. Whenever control passes to that upper box, the execution flow begins at the *Start* symbol within that box. Notice that there is also an arrow leading from the lower inset box to the upper inset box. This means that when the user's session is currently within one of the states anywhere the lower inset box, the user can always choose to return to the upper inset box (although this diagram does not indicate the precise mechanism for doing so.)

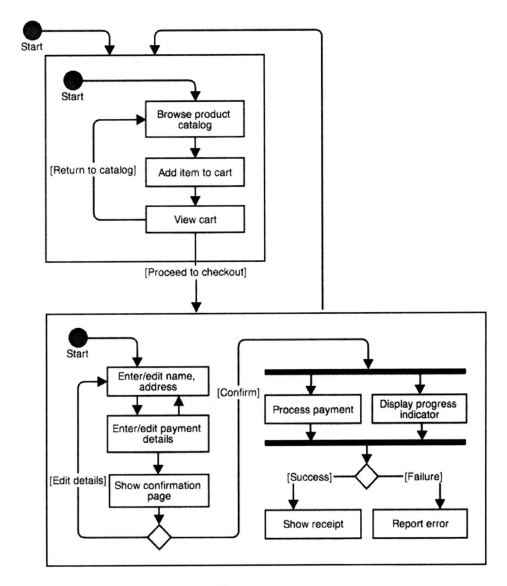

FIGURE 15-7

UML activity diagrams are a powerful tool for both business process modelling and for designing task flows within an application. A complete discussion of all of the notational features of UML activity diagrams is out of the scope of this book. You may wish to consult one of the many guides to the UML standard available, such as *The Unified Modeling Language User Guide* (Booch *et al.*, 2005).

UML 2.0 state machine diagrams

State machine diagrams (also known as **statecharts** or **state transition diagrams**) are diagrams that depict a set of possible states of some aspect of a system, and indicate the allowed transitions between those states. The UML 2.0 definition of state machine diagrams shares some additional notational features that are also present in UML activity diagrams.

State machine diagrams could be used to describe certain types of processes and task flows in an application. They would also be quite suitable for drawing navigation maps.

However, the most frequent use of state machine diagrams is to depict lifecycles or other sets of states and transitions that can be maintained by data model entities. As one example, employee benefits management systems usually need to track the marital status of employees and retirees. A state machine diagram depicting the states and transitions involved in tracking an individual's marital status is given in Figure 15-8.

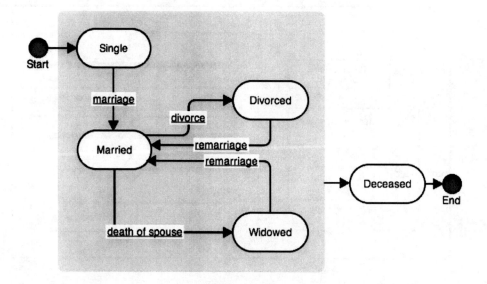

FIGURE 15-8

Behavior tables and event tables

Screen mockups, whether high- or low-fidelity, show which controls will be presented on the screen, but static images alone do not explain how the application will behave when those controls are clicked, pressed, or otherwise activated by the user.

For each mockup of a "place" in the application (i.e., a screen, window, dialog, or page),

204

a **behavior table** can be produced. A behavior table lists all of the controls and visual elements available, and indicates what behavior will result when each one is selected or manipulated. If controls will be enabled or disabled or will or will not appear based on certain conditions, then an additional column can be added to capture that logic. For example, given the following mockup of a simple music player application...

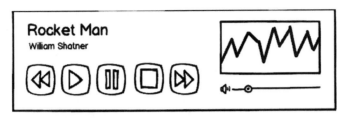

FIGURE 15-9

...we could specify its behavior with a behavior table such as the following:

Control	Control type	Behavior	Visibility and enablement
Play	Button	Starts playback of the current song at the current position.	Always visible; enabled whenever a song is loaded
Stop	Button	Stops playback and resets current position to the beginning of the current song.	Always visible; enabled only when a song playback is currently in progress
Rewind	Button	A single press shall move the current playback position back by ten seconds; pressing and holding the button shall move the current playback position back by ten seconds for each second the button is depressed.	Always visible; enabled only when a song playback is currently in progress
Fast-Forward	Button	A single press shall move the current playback position ahead by ten seconds; pressing and holding the button shall move the current playback position ahead by ten seconds for each second the button is depressed.	Always visible; enabled only when a song playback is currently in progress

Control	Control type	Behavior	Visibility and enablement
Pause	Toggle button	• If a song is playing and this button is pressed, then "paused" mode shall be activated: the playback will be stopped, but the current position will be retained. • If the "paused" mode is active and this button is pressed, then "paused" mode will be deactivated and song playback will resume at the current position.	Always visible; enabled only when a song playback is currently in progress, or when the song playback is currently in "paused" mode
Volume	Slider	Moving the slider shall adjust the volume. If the slider is moved all the way to the left, the volume shall be zero and no sound shall be emitted. If the slider is moved all the way to the right, the volume shall be at its maximum level. If the slider is moved somewhere between, the volume shall be adjusted proportionate to the position.	Always visible and enabled
Song title	Label (read-only)	Displays the title of the current song. If no song is currently loaded, the label will be blank. This is a read-only control; the user cannot edit the song title.	Always visible and enabled, but label may be blank
Artist name	Label (read-only)	Displays the name of the artist of the current song. If no song is currently loaded, the label will be empty. This is a read-only control; the user cannot edit the artist name.	Always visible and enabled, but label may be blank
Oscil-loscope	Graphic display panel (read-only)	This control shall display in real-time the waveform of the audio stream. When song playback is not in progress, a horizontal line shall be displayed.	Always visible and enabled

FIGURE 15-10

Although the behavior table above might seem to imply that all product behavior is triggered by user actions, many applications also have behavior that is triggered by internal system events, external events (such as communications from another system), or timer events. Such event-driven behaviors could then be described in one or more additional **event tables** such as the following:

Event trigger condition	Behavior
Playback of the current song is complete	If there are additional songs remaining in the playlist, then the next song is loaded, the name of the song is updated in the display, and song playback is initiated. The playlist position indicator is updated.
	If there are no additional songs remaining in the playlist, the song title and oscilloscope displays are cleared. The *Play*, *Stop*, *Rewind*, *Fast-Forward*, and *Pause* buttons are disabled (greyed out).

FIGURE 15-11

Some behaviors may be complex (for instance, depending on the states of many different controls or data model objects) and will not fit neatly into a simple table structure. In such cases, additional explanatory prose, tables, or diagrams will be needed.

Validation tables

Most business software applications follow a form-filling metaphor. Data entry screens generally need to enforce validity checks to maintain data integrity and to ensure compliance with business rules.

In some specifications documents, rules for validity checks are scattered throughout the text, which can make it difficult for developers and testers to systematically ensure they have implemented and tested all of the validations. One solution is to add a **validation table** for each place in the application where validations will be performed.

Figure 15-12 gives a simple example of a validations table. It makes the assumption that if there are multiple error conditions, then only the first error detected will be reported. Such assumptions should be stated somewhere in the specification.

Condition	Error message (English-language locale)
The *Export File* checkbox is checked, but no filename has been specified	"Please specify a filename for the file to be exported."
The *Start Date* value for the report is later than today's date	"The start date for the report must be earlier than today's date."

FIGURE 15-12

Chapter 16 discusses additional issues to keep in mind when designing validation and error handling schemes.

While we're on the topic of tables, we should note that tables and matrices are often suitable for many general purposes in software specifications. For applications with complex business logic, for instance, it is common to see things such as business rules or calculation steps specified using tables.

Summary

In this chapter, we've explored a number of techniques that can be useful for exploring design alternatives and for creating and communicating product designs that can then be used by developers and testers for implementation and testing. The choice of techniques you will choose for your project will depend on the nature of the product you are building, the project strategy you have chosen to follow, the skills of the staff on your project team, and, where applicable, the demands of stakeholders such as clients and government regulators. You may also find that you need to experiment with different techniques to find out which ones work best for your project situation.

16

Designing auxiliary and cross-cutting aspects

Every application has some aspects that affect the entire application on a system-wide basis, and despite their importance, these aspects rarely receive much attention during the initial prototyping and design stages of a project. In this chapter, we'll examine the design of some of the most crucial of these aspects, including:

- Error messages and error handling

- Help systems and documentation

- Search systems

- Security

Error messages and error handling

Errors are unexpected or undesirable situations, or violations of data integrity, that prevent the normal operation of the application. We might classify errors by their general types and severities:

- The worst type of error is the **unrecoverable crash**, in which the program abruptly stops due to a programming mistake that usually involves an unforeseen situation. Usually no indication is provided for the cause of the error, although it is virtually always an internal technical detail that would not be comprehensible to general users. Extensive testing, careful code inspections, and the use of static analysis tools can substantially reduce but never completely eliminate the possibility of unrecoverable crashes in complex systems.

- **Technical errors** are errors with an internal cause (i.e., the user is not directly at fault) that prevent some task or action from being completed, or cause data corruption or other unwanted and unexpected behavior, but do not crash the entire application.

- **Transient technical errors** are situations in the application's environment that temporarily hinder the application's proper operation, but which can usually be corrected by taking actions outside of the application. For example, the network connection might be temporarily broken, or a disk may have no free space remaining.

- **Data validation** or **rule violation errors** are situations where the application has detected that a data item, or some combination of data items, does not meet some criteria for validity. The application cannot function correctly as long as the data remains in this state, and so the user is notified, and the user is expected to correct the data.

- **Warnings** are cases where the application detects a real or potential situation that doesn't prevent operation but which could lead to unwanted or unexpected consequences.

We should also note that if the system interacts with other systems or the real world, programming mistakes and invalid data can lead to "error-like situations in the world". For instance, if your application prints out checks but the address on the check or envelope omits the postal code, the envelopes may not be deliverable by the postal system, and the recipients won't receive their checks.

Errors usually occur as a result of the user taking some action, although sometimes a system will report an error out of the blue, for instance, when a background process has encountered a failure, or when a message has been received from another system. Data-entry forms are one of the most common places where errors are identified and presented. In most data-entry forms, the data must be checked for completeness and validity before the task flow can continue.

Presenting errors

Usually, the user is informed of errors by means of **error messages**, which may be presented by means such as pop-up dialogs, lists (when there are multiple errors), status bars, or callout messages alongside fields in a data-entry form.

In some applications, you may be able to indicate errors using highlighting or non-textual symbols. For example, word processors often highlight misspellings with squiggly red underlines, and cells with formatting errors in Microsoft Excel are marked with a colored triangle.

Guidelines for writing error messages

When writing error messages, here are some guidelines to keep in mind:

- Phrase error messages carefully so that the messages clearly identify the problem in a way that your users will understand.

- When possible, explain or give clues as to how to solve the problem. This can be very useful for new users, but can also be seen as cumbersome for more experienced users, especially when the explanations are very detailed. (The IBM DB2 database system's error messages are sometimes over a page long and scroll off the screen!)

- For error messages that contain lengthy explanations, ensure that there's an emphasized headline or summary so that experienced users can identify the error message quickly. This also helps users refer to the error, for instance, if they are talking to a technical support representative.

  Or, you may consider presenting only the brief summary, and then allow the user to click a button to access help content relating to the error.

- Consider the level of abstraction that is suitable for your target audience. Complex software systems are built upon stacked tiers or layers of abstractions, and an error message generated in a low-level component may be too arcane or obscure to be exposed to the user without translation into a more user-friendly form.

  For example, when trying to save information to a database, if a required field is missing, the database might generate an error such as "Cannot insert NULL." This message should not be presented to the user in this form, as it results from a technical situation that the user cannot see and cannot access, and it doesn't pinpoint what or where the actual problem is. It also doesn't give any clues as to how to solve the problem. If the system cannot prevent these types of errors through improved program design, it should catch these errors and relay a more suitable error message, such as "Please enter a value for the *Due Date* field".

- Avoid blaming or criticizing the user. Users can feel ashamed, guilty, or angry when they perceive the system is reprimanding them for a mistake they have made. But more often it is the design of the system that is really at fault. When the error is a system exception and the user is not at fault, the error text should reassure the user that he or she has done nothing wrong. If the error has caused the user some inconvenience, it is courteous to apologize for the error.

Additional suggestions for presenting and handling errors

Here are some more tips and guidelines for handling error situations in your application:

- Let the user correct errors and mistakes easily. Allow the user to undo an operation or retry an action without losing data or having to start over from scratch. For validation errors, allow the user go back and correct the erroneous fields without having to re-enter all of the data on the form.

- For validation errors, whenever possible, show the error messages in close proximity to what is causing the error. If the data in a form field is invalid, try to place either an error indication or the error message alongside the field. Don't put a list of errors on another page or in a pop-up dialog and then expect the user to navigate back to find and correct the errors. However, some validation errors involve multiple fields or multiple information sources, and in these cases, it is not always quite so simple.

- Color can be used to highlight errors (e.g., marking invalid fields with a red border or background), but don't make it the only signal, because it may not be noticeable to visually-impaired or color-blind users.

- One study found that expert users of word processors spend about 30% of their time correcting typographical mistakes (Card *et al.*, 1983). Because of the amount of time spent on error correction, improving the efficiency and ease of correcting errors is often the biggest thing you can do to increase productivity.

- Obviously, whenever possible, try to design the system to use constraints and validations to reduce the number of error conditions that can occur at a later stage. For example, the user may be unsure of the correct format for entering a date value. If you pre-fill the date field with a default date in the correct format, or if you let the user pick the date with a calendar control, there will be fewer chances for the user to enter the format incorrectly.

- Make sure that the user is actually aware of important error messages, by making them visible. For example, some systems display error messages in the status bar at the bottom of the screen, but when the user's focus is elsewhere on the screen, it's not always easy for the user to perceive that the message in the status bar has changed. (Using a status bar for displaying errors also has the problem that it can only show one message at a time, and so multiple errors tend to flicker by faster than they can be read.)

- Non-critical warning messages that are presented repeatedly can quickly become a nuisance. You may wish to offer a "Do not show me this warning again" checkbox for such warnings.

- For transient technical errors such as a broken network connection, the system should attempt to retry the operation several times before generating an error message, unless this is particularly time-consuming.

- Some types of errors and mistakes made by the user could be automatically corrected by the system. Microsoft Word will detect and auto-correct certain spelling mistakes and typos, for example. Some systems will accept dates in virtually any format, and will automatically convert the data to the preferred format when the date is unambiguously recognizable.

  When the system performs an auto-correction, there should be clear but unobtrusive feedback so that the user is aware of the action that has occurred. The user should be able to verify that the correction was in fact correct. You should also offer an option to disable auto-correct behavior, because there is nothing more arduous than repeatedly correcting unwanted auto-corrections.

- Especially for enterprise systems, when a fatal error occurs, you might ask the user to notify the helpdesk. In such cases, you should provide an error ID or reference number so that the helpdesk staff can easily identify the error.

  Often, details about the circumstances of the error are necessary for technicians and developers to properly investigate and diagnose the problem and identify a solution. Stack traces and system configuration details, for instance, may be needed to understand the context and reproduce the error. As a compromise, you may choose to present simplified error messages to users, but then save the technical error messages and contextual data to a log or a database for later inspection by the support team and the developers. The application could also transmit such information electronically. However, if any private or personal data will be saved and transmitted, you will need to ask permission before storing or transmitting it. Ensure that privacy laws involving the use and protection of personal data are respected.

- Some systems must allow invalid or incomplete data to be saved. Prospective students applying to colleges and universities must often submit a number of documents and supporting materials such as transcripts, test scores, and letters of reference, and it may take weeks for the proper documents to be received. Even though some of the required data for a prospective student may be still missing, the enterprise system used for managing the application process will still allow administrators to view, edit, and save applicants' records. Some pension administration systems will even allow administrators to intentionally override certain errors so that preliminary benefit estimates can be calculated even when some information is missing or known to be invalid. And programming environments such as Eclipse allow source code files to be edited and saved, even when they contain syntax errors.

In such systems, a list of outstanding errors is maintained by the system, and all of the errors eventually have to be resolved before some key final task can be completed.

In systems that permit these "persistent" errors, users must be able to easily access and review the list of errors. Ideally, the user should be able to click on an error to navigate to the place where the error can be corrected. And in workflow-driven enterprise systems, reports or alerts should alert staff to any files or cases that have been left hanging without action for a certain length of time.

Dealing with errors is always an unpleasant situation for users. An interface design that minimizes the number of errors presented to users and makes correcting errors easy can greatly improve the user experience.

Help systems and documentation

As designers, we hope to make our products so intuitive and obvious that they can be learned and used without the need for any instructions or help. Yet for non-trivial applications, this is not always possible. Help systems, tutorials, and other forms of documentation can help bridge the so-called **gulf of execution** between the user's intentions to achieve a goal and the user's ability to carry out those intentions, by providing the conceptual understanding and/or step-by-step guidance that users need to be able to complete their tasks.

But do users read documentation? Given the costs involved, is it worth the expense of creating help systems and manuals that users may never look at?

Typically, users won't read documentation except as a last resort. Most users will try to figure things out for themselves. When they get stuck, some users will seek answers in the online help system, and some users will use a search engine to try to find an answer to a particular question. Especially in an office environment, many users will also prefer to ask a peer or coworker for help before consulting any documentation.

Many internal enterprise information system projects make the decision to intentionally skimp on user documentation and help, and instead to provide staff training sessions. Users are then encouraged to contact the helpdesk should questions and problems arise. For mass-market consumer applications and websites, though, training sessions are obviously not a practical option, and it is much more economically sensible to invest in providing useful and usable help and documentation rather than increasing the demands on the customer support department.

In thinking about what forms of documentation you will provide to your users, consider both the medium and content:

- **Medium:** Printed manuals, standalone electronic manuals (such as PDF files), an integrated online help system in the application, web-based documentation, video material, live training, physical quick reference cards, or some combination of these?

- **Content:** Quick-start guides, tutorials and walkthroughs, "teach yourself" manuals that explain fundamental concepts, reference handbooks, Frequently Asked Questions (FAQ) lists, or some combination of these?

To decide on what is suitable for your product, let's consider the following questions: How do users use documentation and help systems? When and how do users access these information sources? And what are they looking for?

Revisiting the range of user skill levels, we can imagine the following general use cases:

- New or prospective users who are evaluating the application will need to find out what the application is capable of doing and whether it will meet their needs.

- Beginning users will often need step-by-step instructions on how to get started with the application. Beginning users who are experimenting with performing a task but get stuck will seek answers as to how to continue and successfully complete the task.

- Intermediate or experienced users who have performed a task in the past but who have now forgotten how to do it will seek just enough information to serve as a memory-refreshing reminder.

- Some intermediate or experienced users will seek out tips and tricks for improving productivity, such as keyboard shortcuts.

- Some applications, like spreadsheets and programming environments, may offer a large set of commands and functions with complex options, and users will want to look up reference information such as the proper syntax, details of arguments, and examples of usage.

With these use cases in mind, here are some general guidelines for designing an online help system and creating help content and documentation:

- Help systems should be **context-sensitive**. In other words, when the user opens the help system, instead of simply showing a table of contents, it should display content relevant to the task the user is doing or the place (the screen, page, dialog, or tab) where the user is currently situated.

- Users are usually accessing on-line help when they don't know how to get started with a new task, or when they get lost or confused and need guidance to get back on track. Keep help topics short, focused, and highly structured; when information on performing tasks can be presented as a concrete, step-by-step procedure, it should be presented this way.

- Understand the skill level and existing domain knowledge of your users, and use standard vocabulary that they will understand. If completing a task requires background understanding that you suspect the user might not have (because they wouldn't need to access the help had they known this background information), then you may wish to offer a link to supplementary help topics or introductory guides that define the necessary terminology and explain the fundamental concepts.

- When referring to elements, controls, tasks, and places, be sure to consistently employ the standard names you've chosen for use throughout the application. For example, refer to the "Find" dialog consistently with that name, rather than calling it by various alternative names like "Find/Replace", "Find & Replace", or "Search and Replace".

- Examples can help illustrate a procedure, but on the other hand, don't force the user to follow along with an elaborate, extended example than spans multiple help topics or reference manual chapters.

- Flipping back and forth between help text and the interface can be annoying. If possible, allow the help text window and application window to exist side-by-side so that the user can follow a procedure without having to switch back and forth. Pop-up callouts that give help for specific controls can also be used to avoid this problem.

- Consider allowing users to bookmark content in the help system or online documentation that they plan to access frequently.

- Some users like to print out help content, as having instructions on a sheet of paper can be more convenient than flipping between a help system window and the application, and the paper can be marked up with notes. Having a printed page on the desk or pinned to the cubicle wall might be considered an external, physical form of bookmarking.

- In help systems and online documentation, provide reliable search functionality and a good index. Providing search doesn't alleviate the need for an index, because searching is only practical when the user knows the right word or phrase to search for. When the user doesn't know the right term or cannot recall it, scanning an index can be useful. Be sure to **rotate** phrases (e.g., list both "keyboard shortcuts" and "shortcuts, keyboard" in the index) and provide synonyms (e.g., "keyboard short-cuts", "keyboard commands", "command keys", etc.) so that users can more easily find what they are specifically looking for.

- A hierarchical table of contents or a list of help topics can give users an overview of what material is available.

- Providing screenshots can be very useful for visually explaining how to complete a procedure. However, beware that screenshots may not fit in the window if the help system window is resized to appear alongside the application.

  Note also that during product development and maintenance, you will need a change control process so that screenshots are kept synchronized with all user interface changes. Managing multiple versions of screenshots can also be tricky when dealing with multiple languages and locales, or multiple platforms and operating systems.

- Be sure that the help content actually answers the questions that users will have. For example, one secure e-mail application required the user to choose an encryption standard from a list that included names similar to "800X", "424A", and "335B". Non-technical users would not know which one to choose, and the help content in this particular system was not of much assistance: For the "800X" radio button, the help text simply said, "Selects the 800X standard"; for "424A", it said, "Selects the 424A standard", and so on. What the user was really looking for was guidance on how to choose one of these standards. An explanation of the benefits and risks of each one, and a discussion of interoperability issues (e.g., does the receiver of the e-mail have to have the same settings?), would have been more helpful here.

- In help systems and online documentation, it can be useful to provide navigation links (e.g., "See also...") to related help topics and sections.

- Use analytics and usability testing to find out what your users' biggest problems are, and what help content is being accessed most frequently. When you observe users using your application, where do they have the most trouble? What keywords are people searching for and what problems are people asking about on support forums? If your website or application tracks and submits usage data and error reports, what are the contexts in which these errors are occurring? Use these findings to improve the help content.

- You can collect feedback on the help content and documentation from users, by providing submission forms for comments, and by asking questions such as "Was this useful? (1-5 stars)". Such feedback can be valuable in identifying what content needs improvement.

- If your help content and other documentation is hosted on the web, you can allow users to contribute to it. The most extreme form of this is to make your help system a wiki that anybody can edit, and of course this has advantages and disadvantages. Both petty vandals and well-intentioned contributors who submit incorrect information can quickly degrade the usefulness and trustworthiness of the documentation. Wikis also tend to become sloppy and jumbled from contributions from multiple authors. Inconsistent formatting and writing styles and broken links should be addressed via regular maintenance and editing by a curator or moderator.

  A more practical approach may be to allow users to *add* comments. The PHP programming language and the MySQL database system are examples of products with reference documentation sets that allow users to add comments at the end of each page. Often these comments are very useful, with users providing sample code or clarifying practical issues. Often contributors point out deficiencies and errors in the original documentation, and write complaints about deficiencies and inconsistencies in the design of the product. In some cases, errors have gone uncorrected for years; for a private company, this could be embarrassing, and so you should allocate resources to moderating the comments and updating the documentation.

- Community-driven question-and-answer sites like Stack Overflow are an increasingly popular way of facilitating structured interactive discussions about problems and questions. You might consider creating such a site for your product.

Search systems

The design and the quality of the search functionality in document- and content-oriented applications and websites can greatly impact the ability of users to navigate and to find the information they are looking for.

In a typical search scenario, the user enters a search query, and in response, the system presents a list of matching items or documents from a repository.

Alternatively, you might think of searching as a form of filtering mechanism: The user chooses filter criteria, and the system filters out all of the items that do not match those criteria.

When you're designing a search system, consider the following:

- What types of items are in the repository to be searched? Files, documents, images, videos, database records? Can the search return multiple types of items?

- What is the form of the search query? Is it a simple keyword search, or are there multiple fields, checkboxes, and drop-down lists that act as filter criteria? And will you provide "basic" and "advanced" search interfaces to cater to the needs of different user audiences? (See Figure 16-1.)

FIGURE 16-1

- If it is a textual search, does it search for an exact phrase match? Is it case sensitive?

- What is the *scope* of the search? For example, when searching documents, are matches for the search term sought only in the text of the document, or are metadata such as the filename, document title, document properties, and tags searched as well?

- If you support features such as wildcards, regular expressions, or boolean operators (AND, OR, and NOT), how will you communicate to the user that these features are available, and where will you explain the proper syntax and the order of operations? Google's *Advanced Search* page, depicted in Figure 16-2, offers many options like these, and presents the syntax using explanatory hints:

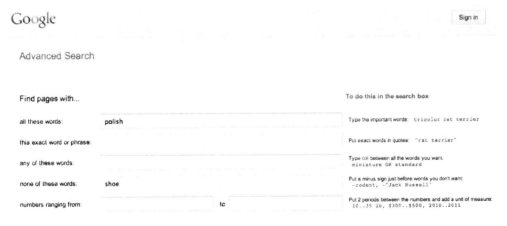

FIGURE 16-2

- Does the search attempt to find appropriate variations of the search term? Will the technique of **stemming** be employed so that a search for "eat" also finds instances of inflected forms like "eats", "eating", "eaten", and "ate"?

- How are search results presented? When the user submits a search query, are the results presented on a separate page? Or are the results presented on the same screen and filtered in real-time as the user modifies the search criteria? If there are many results, will the results be broken up across multiple pages, and how will the navigation be presented for this (see Figure 16-3)?

FIGURE 16-3

- If the search results are textual documents, is a small snippet of the text surrounding the match presented to provide context? What if there are multiple matches within the same document? (Figure 16-4 shows how this is handled by Google.)

Puppies, Cute Puppy Names, Pictures of Puppies & More | Daily ...
www.dailypuppy.com/
Find cute **puppy** pictures and videos. Learn how to care for and train **puppies**. Submit your **puppy** to be the daily **puppy**, create profiles for you and your dogs and ...
↳ Dogs - Pupfolio - Photos - Puppy Showdown

Puppies for Sale, Dogs for Sale and Dog Breeders
www.puppyfind.com/
Directory of dog breeders with **puppies** for sale and dogs for adoption. Find the right breed, and the perfect **puppy** at PuppyFind.com.
↳ Find a Puppy - Member Login - English Bulldog Puppies for Sale - Great Dane

Dogs & Puppies - Cats & Kittens - Pets for Sale at Pets4Homes UK
www.pets4homes.co.uk/
Find Dogs, **Puppies**, Cats, Kittens for sale at the UKs most popular free pet advertising site for pedigree and non pedigree dogs, **puppies**, cats, kittens and other ...

FIGURE 16-4

- Can users save and retrieve search queries that they expect to use frequently?

Search quality

The perceived quality of search results is a function of the following factors:

- **Accuracy of recall:** Search results exhibit high *recall accuracy* if the results *include* all of the items that match the search criteria, and *exclude* all of the items that do not match the search criteria. If the search does not locate all of the matching items, or if irrelevant items are presented, the inaccurate results can mislead the user. It can be especially frustrating if the user is searching for something that he or she knows exists, but the search system cannot find it.

- **Relevance:** It's desirable to sort the results to show the most relevant items first, although the definition of relevance depends on the application. More recent news articles would be expected to be presented ahead of older articles, for instance, and an article featuring multiple instances of the search phrase would typically be considered more relevant than an article that mentioned the phrase only once in passing, or in a different context. Having to dig through "noisy" results to find relevant items is annoying and time-consuming.

- **Performance:** Search results should be delivered promptly. For systems with extremely large repositories of data, building search systems that are both performant and cost-effective can be a challenge.

Lookups

A specialized form of search functionality is the **lookup** function sometimes associated with certain data-entry fields. For example, a customer number field might allow the user to enter a customer number directly, but there may be tens of thousands of customers on file, and it is not reasonable to expect the user to know all of the customer numbers. In such cases, the field should provide a lookup button (or a shortcut keystroke) that allows the user to search for a customer by name. Upon selection of a customer, the customer number field is then populated with the corresponding customer number.

Finding text within a document

In document-based applications like word processors and web browsers, users will expect to be able to find all of the instances of a search term within the current document. (The generally-accepted terminology in English-language software is to *search* to locate instances of a term within a repository of documents, and to *find* to locate instances of a term within an individual document.) For editable documents, the ability to replace instances of the search term with another term will also be expected.

Security

Security is a critical requirement in many software and web applications, but security measures often are seen as annoyances that negatively impact the user experience. The essential purpose of security, however, is to protect users and other stakeholders from more serious negative experiences.

For example, having to remember a complex password can be annoying. But it reduces the chances of more unpleasant and dangerous experiences occurring, such as losing access to your account, having your data stolen, deleted, or tampered with, having fraudulent transactions conducted on your behalf, or having someone impersonate you.

Thus, like so many issues in software design, there is a trade-off between security measures and usability. Let's survey some common security mechanisms and issues and examine them from a usability perspective.

Authentication

Authentication refers to the process of *identifying* the user and *verifying* that they really are who they say they are.

To gain access to a system, a user must prove that he or she is someone who has been granted permission to access that system, and this is done by providing proof of identity. Most systems implement this by **challenging** the user to provide a username and password. The username can exist only if an account has been granted to a particular approved person, and, in theory, only that person should know the password for the account. And so by providing the correct password, the user is "proving" that they are who they say they are.

Since username-and-password pairs can be guessed or stolen, they are a weak means of identification, but passwords persist because they are cheap and easy to implement. Physical tokens like ID badges or keycards, or biometric identification using fingerprints or retinal scans, are alternative but costlier means of identification.

Stronger security can be achieved by combining physical tokens or biometric identification together with a password. For example, a bank card and a PIN (personal identification number) are required in order to withdraw money from a bank machine. If one of the two halves is compromised (either the card is stolen or the PIN is discovered), the thief or hacker still cannot gain access to the bank account.

Short passwords can be easily guessed or cracked using brute-force algorithms, so requiring passwords to be of a certain minimum length, and requiring passwords to include characters from an extended character set (numbers, punctuation symbols, etc.) can greatly reduce the chances of hackers gaining illicit access. Complex passwords come at the cost of irritating users, though, who quite understandably have a hard time remembering the passwords for all of the systems and websites they interact with.

Likewise, a requirement for users to change their passwords every few months is recommended by security experts, but users tend to resent this added memorization burden.

The strictness of the security requirements should match what is at stake. An Internet discussion forum does not require the same security as a banking website, and a banking website might not require the same measures needed for a classified military installation.

Security violations like intrusions and leaked passwords are highly embarrassing, and so your product's technical architects must ensure that they are employing current best practices for implementing the security system. Security audits are worthwhile if your organization can afford them.

In enterprise information systems, applications are often constructed in **integration projects** by cobbling together several commercial off-the-shelf (COTS) products. It is highly unpleasant if the user has to log in with separate usernames and passwords every day to access the constituent products (such as a Customer Relationship Management application, a workflow application, and a reporting tool) that make up the system. A **single sign-on** solution is recommended for such systems so that a single login grants the user access to all of the constituent products.

Automatically logging out the user after a period of inactivity is a measure designed to reduce somewhat the chances of a malicious user taking over a user's session should the user leave the machine unattended. To reduce annoyance, however, the timeout period should not be so short that the user will be logged out during normal operation, and when after the user logs in again, the system should resume where it left off.

Authorization (access control)

Authorization, also known as **access control**, refers to controlling what each particular user is allowed to access. Which functions are permitted, and which functions are prohibited? What information can be viewed and edited, and what information is off-limits?

Rather than controlling access to individual users, most systems define **roles**. Users can then be assigned to one or more roles. An **access control matrix**, such as the following, can then be created to define what functions the members of each role are permitted to access:

Functions	Roles		
	Teller	Loan Officer	Manager
Process withdrawal	yes	no	yes
Process deposit	yes	no	yes
Process mortgage application	no	yes	yes
Approve mortgage	no	yes	yes
Override interest rate	no	no	yes

FIGURE 16-5

A key decision to be made involves the presentation of the menu items and buttons for functions that the current user is prohibited from accessing. Should these controls be shown in a disabled state (i.e., greyed out), or should they be hidden completely?

- With *greyed-out controls*, it might not always be obvious to the user that the reason why the control is greyed out is because of an access control restriction. Users in some cases might think that the application is simply in the wrong mode, for instance, and might waste time trying to figure out actions needed to re-enable the controls.

- *Hiding controls* can be an attractive option because it produces less clutter, but it can also cause confusion if a user is looking for something that he or she had seen before (perhaps while watching a coworker use the application), and now it can no longer be found. Hiding controls can also cause layout issues; if the layout is static, there will be empty gaps where the controls used to be, and if the layout is dynamic, the remaining controls will shift their positions, making the alignment of controls for the purpose of presenting a clean visual design more difficult. Additionally, the same screen will appear differently when users with different roles log in, and so if you include screenshots in the documentation and help content, the screenshots might not match what the user is actually looking at.

Fraud prevention

Enterprise systems that deal with financial transactions often must consider fraud prevention. If a user can issue a payment to a customer, for instance, what would stop a user from creating a customer account for herself and then issuing herself a few payments?

224

If the system is structured so that payment transactions must be reviewed and approved by a peer coworker or a manager (this is sometimes called the **two-man rule** or the **four-eyes principle**), and if all transactions are permanently recorded and logged, then this kind of fraud is less likely to occur, as there is a risk of getting caught and reported if someone were to seek out a collaborator, and there is a permanent record (an **audit trail**) of the fraudulent activity.

17

Usability testing and evaluation

Given a user interface design, whether a prototype or a full-fledged product, how can you judge whether it will meet your users' needs and whether it is sufficiently usable? There are many ways to test and evaluate the usability of a design, and this chapter will explain the most practical and effective techniques. Before we explore those techniques, though, it is a good idea to have a clear idea of what your goals are and what kind of information you seek.

Choosing goals for usability evaluation sessions

Before conducting a usability evaluation, decide in advance what kind of data or learnings you are aiming to get. This will help determine what methods are appropriate, and by setting goals, you are more likely to stay on track and general useful and actionable research results.

For instance, in evaluating a design prototype or an actual product, you may want to:

- determine what percentage of users are able to carry out a task successfully;

- find places or situations where users get confused, hesitate, or don't know to proceed;

- find places or situations where users tend to make the most errors;

- find places or situations where users consult documentation or on-line help;

- collect impressions and suggestions from users on what works well and what could be improved;

- collect judgments from users on the value, usefulness, attractiveness, and usability of the product and its features; or

- get feedback on how your product compares with competing products.

Evaluation techniques can also be used to collect **usability metrics**, which will let you quantitatively compare alternatives, or detect and monitor trends over multiple design iterations. If you count or measure, say, the average number of errors users make, or the average time taken to perform a task, you can compare the statistics across different iterations and testing sessions to determine whether the changes to the product have actually led to measurable improvements. Chapter 6 provides a list of metrics that you may wish to consider measuring and tracking.

Evaluation techniques

Let's now examine some of the most popular and effective usability evaluation techniques.

User observation

User observation sessions involve watching real users as they operate your product or prototype. User observation is generally the most effective way to truly evaluate whether your design is sufficiently usable and learnable, and can quickly reveal where users have problems figuring out your product. Let's take a look at running effective user observation sessions.

The environment

Some textbooks recommend setting up a formal usability testing lab with one-way mirrors and multiple cameras, and they recommend that you run highly structured sessions with a full team of facilitators, observers and recorders. If you can afford this, then it is something you might consider, but these ideas make user observation seem more complicated and mysterious than it really is.

Not only are formal laboratory environments expensive, but they can make participants feel uncomfortable. Being watched by a team of people and being recorded by cameras will give most participants performance anxiety.

To make people feel more relaxed, you can get great results simply by sitting one-on-one with a participant in front of a laptop in a meeting room, or even in a coffee shop. If you're building a product that will be used in a particular environment, try to carry out the session in that environment: If you're building enterprise software, sit down together at your users' actual desks. If you're building software for police officers on patrol, schedule meetings with officers in their police cars. Not only are people are more likely to open up and discuss their opinions more freely when they're in familiar surroundings, but you'll also get a better feeling for the environment and the context of the work.

Depending on your goals and budget, you may consider recording the interaction with screen recording software and an audio recorder. Possibly, you might also consider setting up a camera to record the user's body language, facial reactions, and physical interactions with input devices. But you need to be aware that people act differently when they know they are being recorded. And while recording a session offers the convenience of replaying and reanalyzing the recording as many times as you like, you should also not underestimate the amount of time it will take to review and analyze a batch of recordings.

Running the session

When you start a session, welcome the participant and briefly explain what goals you're aiming to accomplish. If you will be conducting audio, video, or screen recording of the session, or if any personally identifying data will be collected, it is customary to have the participant understand and agree to this by signing a consent form.

How you run the session depends on what data you're intending to collect. Typically, you will ask the user to accomplish one or more goals, and you'll observe the user as he or she explores the product and attempts to figure out how to go about achieving those goals. Make sure you explain the goals or tasks clearly, but at the same time, try not to give too many clues as to how to do it ("leading" the user). If you tell the user precisely how to carry out a task, you won't learn very much.

Users will often ask for help or seek acknowledgement that they're on the right track, asking questions such as, "Is this right? Do I press this? What's the next step?" How you offer assistance is up to you. When the user makes a false step, you may be tempted to jump in right away, but it's better to observe how the user attempts to recover from the error.

Because they are being observed, participants often feel that they are being tested or quizzed, and participants can often become embarrassed and ashamed when they make a mistake or can't figure out how to do something with the product. Reassure subjects that you're not testing or evaluating them personally; instead, you're testing and evaluating the product, and because the product is not yet perfect or complete, the goal is to find flaws and opportunities for improvement in the product. Explain that if the participant makes an error or gets stuck, it's not his or her fault; rather, it's a signal that the product might need to be improved.

You can ask for critiques and suggestions at various stages, and you should carefully listen to and record all of the feedback that participants offer. At the same time, realize that different participants will likely have conflicting opinions and ideas, and while it is important to know what users think, not all of their feedback necessarily has to be incorporated into the product.

The think-aloud protocol

A useful technique to employ is the **think-aloud protocol**, in which you ask participants to verbalize their inner thought processes as they go about their tasks. So as participants try to figure out how the product works, they tell a narrative of what they are thinking: "I want to do a search for something. Where can I do a search? I don't see a search box anywhere. Normally it would be up in this corner over here. Maybe there's something under one of the menus? Hmmm, no, there's no *Search* menu. Maybe under the *Edit* menu? I see a *Find* command, but is that what I want?"

This kind of ongoing dialogue can provide some very useful insights. Unfortunately, many people find it uncomfortable and unnatural to do this when somebody else is watching, and some people are fearful of making a mistake. Talking also slows down and distracts the participant.

Audio or video recording equipment is usually used during sessions that use the think-aloud protocol, as if you're trying to take notes by hand, it's generally impossible to write quickly enough to keep up.

Recording notes and observations

Even if you're using recording equipment, you will want to have a notepad handy for taking notes. You may wish to keep a log of the user's actions, results, comments, questions, any long pauses indicating confusion, and so on. You may also want to keep a tally of events such as errors and mistakes. If you begin to see patterns emerging across multiple observation sessions — for example, users getting stuck or asking how to proceed at a certain point — make a note and keep count of how many other participants encounter the same difficulty. Once you've gained experience with running observation sessions, you might be able to save time by preparing a template or chart you can fill out, and you might develop a list of short abbreviated codes to use to refer to recurring situations.

If you're working with a high-fidelity prototype or the actual product, you might also use a stopwatch to time how long it takes a user to complete certain tasks. However, accurate timings are difficult if you've asked the user to think aloud, if questions and discussions are taking place, or if the user is pausing to let you take notes. Using a stopwatch will also put pressure on users, so again, reassure users that it's not a race and that you're not testing their personal performance.

If you find that your notetaking slows down the session, you may consider having another person join to take notes so you can concentrate on facilitating the session. But having multiple people managing the session can sometimes be distracting and overwhelming. It can also sometimes appear unprofessional if the team members haven't prepared and rehearsed their coordination ahead of time.

Afterwards

Be sure to thank your participant for their time and feedback. You might also ask participants to fill out a questionnaire afterwards. This gives you another chance to collect feedback (and it might give participants more time to reflect on the session).

Analyzing and communicating results

After running a batch of sessions, consolidate your notes and review any recordings. Tally and calculate any metrics, and compare any statistics to previous runs. By analyzing your notes and data, you can find problem areas, for which you can then recommend potential solutions.

Finally, put together the results and recommendations in a brief report or presentation for review and discussion with your project team.

Cognitive walkthrough

The **cognitive walkthrough** technique (Wharton *et al.*, 1994) can be an effective means of detecting many kinds of usability defects with somewhat less effort and expense than is required for conducting user observation sessions. A cognitive walkthrough can be carried out by a single evaluator or can be conducted in a group setting.

To conduct a cognitive walkthrough, you must first choose a task scenario. Choose a typical goal that a user of your application might have, and then write out the sequence of actions needed to carry out the tasks in order to achieve the goal. This list of actions should generally be the "optimal" sequence that an average experienced user would use. (If there are multiple valid and equally efficient ways to complete a task, you might evaluate each as a separate scenario.)

You should then select a user profile and persona. You will role-play as a member of this group who is using the application for the first time.

Then, you simply step through the sequence of actions, and for each action, you inspect the product or prototype and ask several questions, which we will examine shortly. When asking each question, you should frame it in the context of the chosen user profile.

The questions are based around the idea that most users learn to use an application by exploration (rather than reading documentation), and the questions test how well a new user will be able to discover each step in the proper action sequence. The answers to the questions often reveal weaknesses and opportunities for improvement.

The four questions originally recommended by Wharton *et al.* in the first description of the cognitive walkthrough technique are:

1. **"Will the user try to achieve the right effect?"**

   In other words, does the user know the next general step needed to move along the path to achieving the goal?

2. **"Will the user notice that the correct action is available?"**

   Is the appropriate control visible, or is the mechanism of action (such as a touch-screen swiping gesture, or dragging-and-dropping an object) clearly evident?

3. **"Will the user associate the correct action with the effect they are trying to achieve?"**

   Even if the appropriate control is visible, a user may not necessarily be able to make the connection that the control is the correct one to use to accomplish the action. Most users tend to follow a "label-following" strategy, seeking labels that match descriptions of the action they want to accomplish (for example, a user wanting to print a document will probably look for a button or menu option containing the word "Print", or, failing that, a visual depiction of a printer or the act of printing). Is the control marked with a clear and descriptive label or icon so that the effect of the control is evident?

4. **"If the correct action is performed, will the user see that progress is being made toward solution of their task?"**

   Does the application provide appropriate feedback to let the user understand that the action was completed successfully (or unsuccessfully) and to see the results or effects of the action?

Some evaluators find the four questions to be too arduous and time-consuming, and so the walkthrough is sometimes streamlined by focusing primarily on questions 2 and 4, which test for visibility and feedback.

There are some limitations to the cognitive walkthrough method:

- It does not test the interface with real users, and so the assumptions of the evaluators can lead to different results than tests with real users.

- Evaluators using the technique, depending on their rigor, sometimes find an excessive number of usability defects, not all of which are actual problems that users may encounter.

- It tends to be biased in favor of the ease of learning for new users over the efficiency of use for expert users.

Analytics

Once your product has been released, understanding how it is actually being used in the field is very valuable. **Analytics** refers to the use of instrumentation to record data on users' activities, followed by the analysis the collected data to detect trends and patterns. This data can then validate your assumptions as to which functions are being used most frequently and which parts of the product are seldom or never used. The data may also be able to identify places where users are running into trouble.

Some examples of the type of data that you can collect through analytics include:

- Pages or screens visited, and the time spent on each

- Functions used, buttons and controls pressed, menu options selected, shortcut keystrokes pressed, etc.

- Errors and failures
- Duration of usage sessions

Websites and web apps are well suited to logging and tracking user activities. Many web analytics packages and services can provide additional contextual data such as the user's geographic location, whether they have visited the site before, and what search terms were used to find the site if the user visited via a search engine.

Desktop and mobile apps can also collect usage data, but because of privacy concerns and regulations, it is important to declare to the user what data you intend to collect, and you must gain the user's permission before transmitting any usage data.

No matter what type of product you offer, privacy concerns are important and you must ensure that your practices and Terms of Service follow the legal regulations appropriate for your jurisdiction. It's generally acceptable to track abstract usage data such as button presses and page visits, but it is usually considered unacceptable to pry into personal data or any private, unpublished content that a user might create with your product.

Focus groups

A **focus group** brings together a group of users or other stakeholders to participate in a discussion of pre-prepared questions, led by a facilitator. A focus group could be used as an usability evaluation technique if the group is shown a demonstration of a product or prototype, and then the group's impressions and opinions are discussed.

Focus groups might appear to be a convenient, time-saving way to get feedback from as many as eight or ten people in a single session. In practice, however, the technique is not consistently reliable. Watching a demonstration of a product is not the same as having the opportunity to interact with the product hands-on. And group dynamics can vary widely; different groups can come up with completely different conclusions.

Focus group discussions often tend to be dominated by one or two loud and opinionated participants. The quieter participants often say little and simply go along with the group consensus. There is also the risk that the facilitator may consciously or unconsciously lead the discussion towards a particular outcome. If you choose to use focus groups, you should use them with caution and be aware of the limitations.

Questionnaire surveys

At the conclusion of a user observation session or focus group, you might ask participants to fill out a survey. This is an additional chance for participants to reflect on their experience and provide feedback, in written form, about their opinions and suggestions for improving the product.

You can collect quantitative data as well, by counting the responses to true-or-false questions, or by asking for satisfaction ratings on a numerical scale, usually from 1 to 10 (this is known as a **Likert scale**), and computing the average. Numerical data can also be gleaned from textual responses. For example, you could judge each participant's response to be generally positive or negative, and determine the percentage of positive or negative responses. Or you could count the number of times a word or concept, such as "error" or "mistake", is mentioned in the responses.

Numerical metrics are useful for tracking progress over multiple iterations of your product: you can measure whether error rates are increasing or decreasing, for instance, or you can also use numerical metrics to set targets and goals.

Heuristic inspections

Heuristics are "rule-of-thumb" design principles, rules, and characteristics that are stated in broad terms and are often difficult to specify precisely. Assessing whether a product exhibits the qualities embodied in a heuristic is thus a subjective judgment.

If you inspect a prototype or product and systematically decide whether it adheres to a checklist of heuristics, you are conducting what is called a **heuristic inspection** or **heuristic evaluation**. It is a simple, effective, and inexpensive means of identifying problems and defects, and is an excellent first technique to use before moving on to more costly and involved methods such as user observation sessions.

It is usually best when heuristic evaluations are carried out by experienced usability specialists, but heuristic evaluations can also be effective when they are conducted by a team of individuals with diverse backgrounds (for example, domain experts, developers, and users).

To conduct a heuristic evaluation, first choose a set of heuristics, and then choose one or more task scenarios that users will perform. As you act out each of the steps in a scenario, consult the set of heuristics, and judge whether the design of the interface conforms to each heuristic (if it is applicable).

Jakob Nielsen introduced the idea of heuristic evaluations, and his 1994 list of ten heuristics, reproduced in Figure 17-1 below, is still the most commonly used set of heuristics today (Nielsen, 1994, p. 30):

Heuristic	Description
Visibility of system status	"The system should always keep users informed about what is going on, through appropriate feedback within reasonable time."
Match between system and the real world	"The system should speak the user's language, with words, phrases and concepts familiar to the user, rather than system-oriented terms. Follow real-world conventions, making information appear in a natural and logical order."
User control and freedom	"Users often choose system functions by mistake and will need a clearly marked 'emergency exit' to leave the unwanted state without having to go through an extended dialog. [The system] supports undo and redo."
Consistency and standards	"Users should not have to wonder whether different words, situations, or actions mean the same thing. Follow platform conventions."
Error prevention	"Even better than a good error message is a careful design that prevents a problem from occurring in the first place."
Recognition rather than recall	"Make objects, actions, and options visible. The user should not have to remember information from one part of the dialog to another. Instructions or use of the system should be visible or easily retrievable whenever appropriate."
Flexibility and efficiency of use	"Accelerators — unseen by the novice user — may often speed up the interaction for the expert user such that the system can cater to both inexperienced and experienced users. Allow users to tailor frequent actions."
Aesthetic and minimalist design	"Dialogs should not contain information that is irrelevant or rarely needed. Every extra unit of information in a dialog competes with the relevant units of information and diminishes their relative visibility."
Help users recognize, diagnose, and recover from errors	"Error messages should be expressed in plain language (no codes), precisely indicate the problem, and constructively suggest a solution."

Heuristic	Description
Help and documentation	"Even though it is better if the system can be used without documentation, it may be necessary to provide help and documentation. Any such information should be easy to search, focused on the user's task, list concrete steps to be carried out, and not be too large."

FIGURE 17-1

By judging the system against such heuristics, you can generate a list of potential usability problems and product flaws, and you can revise your product design to address those issues.

An obvious weakness of the heuristic evaluation technique is that the inspectors are not the actual users of the system. Biases, pre-existing knowledge, and incorrect assumptions about how users go about tasks are all factors that can skew the results of a heuristic evaluation.

Note that heuristic evaluations can also be combined with **standards inspections** or **checklist inspections**, where you inspect the interface and verify that it conforms to documents such as style guides, platform standards guides, or other specific checklists devised by your project team. This can help ensure conformity and consistency throughout your application.

Acting on results

Once you have collected and analyzed data from one or more usability evaluation techniques, you can begin to make conclusions and decide on what changes to the product design would solve any identified issues. You will want to communicate your findings and recommendations to your project team and any interested stakeholders, and this could be done via a written report or a presentation.

Any issues and the measures to address them should then be prioritized.

In subsequent iterations of your product or prototype, you can then modify the design to address the highest-priority items, implement the updated design, and then re-evaluate the revised product.

If you find that your evaluations themselves are not effective, then you should also analyze the methods you're using and either make necessary changes or experiment with different techniques in the next iteration.

This iterative approach helps ensure that your designs and processes are continually improving, and this is a key approach for ensuring that your products are in fact usable and meeting the needs of your users and stakeholders.

Conclusion

And this concludes *Designing Usable Apps*! I hope you've enjoyed the book and gained some knowledge and ideas that you can apply in your projects.

I'd welcome your feedback, comments, and suggestions on how the next edition of this book can be made better.

You can reach me by e-mail at **kevin@winchelseasystems.com**.

I wish you the best of luck creating software that your users will love.

Kevin Matz

References and bibliography

Aspelund, K. (2010) *The design process*, New York: Fairchild Books.

Barnum, C.M. (2002) *Usability testing and research*, New York: Pearson Education.

Booch, G., Rumbaugh, J., and Jacobson, I. (2005) *The Unified Modeling Language user guide (2e)*, Upper Saddle River, NJ: Addison-Wesley Professional (Pearson Education).

Card, S.K., Moran, T.P. and Newell, A. (1983) *The psychology of human-computer interaction*, Hillsdale, NJ: Lawrence Erlbaum Associates.

Cockburn, A. (2000) *Writing effective use cases*, Addison-Wesley Professional.

Cooper, A., Reimann, R. and Cronin, D. (2007) *About Face 3: The essentials of interaction design*, Indianapolis: Wiley.

Courage, C. and Baxter, K. (2005) *Understanding your users: A practical guide to user requirements; methods, tools, and techniques*, San Francisco: Morgan Kaufmann.

Csikszentmihalyi, M. (1991) *Flow: The psychology of optimal experience*, HarperCollins.

Holzinger, A. (2005) 'Usability engineering methods for software developers' in *Communications of the ACM*, Vol. 48, Issue 1, January 2005.

Jackson, M. (1995) *Software requirements & specifications: A lexicon of practice, principles and prejudices*, New York: ACM Press/Addison-Wesley.

Jackson, M. (2001) *Problem frames: Analyzing and structuring software development problems*, New York: Addison-Wesley.

Jacobson, I., Spence, I., and Bittner, K. (2011) *Use-Case 2.0: The guide to succeeding with use cases*, Ivar Jacobson International SA.

Krug, S. (2000) *Don't make me think!*, New Riders Press.

Kuniavsky, M. (2003) *Observing the user experience: A practitioner's guide to user research*, San Francisco: Morgan Kaufmann.

Lacey, M. (2012) *The Scrum field guide: Practical advice for your first year*, Addison-Wesley Professional.

Miller, G.A. (1956) 'The magical number seven, plus or minus two: Some limits on our capacity for processing information' in *Psychological Review*, Vol. 63, Issue 2, pp. 81–97.

Morville, P. and Rosenfeld, L. (2006) *Information architecture for the world wide web (3e)*, Sebastopol, CA: O'Reilly.

Nielsen, J. (1994) 'Heuristic evaluation' in *Usability inspection methods*, Nielsen, J., and Mack, R.L. (eds.), New York: John Wiley & Sons.

Nielsen, J., and Pernice, K. (2009) *Eyetracking web usability*, New Riders.

Norman, D.A. (1990) *The design of everyday things*, New York: Basic Books.

Olivé, A. (2007) *Conceptual modeling of information systems*, Berlin: Springer-Verlag.

Palmer, S.E. (1992) 'Common region: a new principle of perceptual grouping' in *Cognitive Psychology*, July 1992, 24(3), pp. 436-7.

Raskin, J. (2000) *The humane interface: New directions for designing interactive systems*, Addison-Wesley Professional.

Ries, E. (2011) *The Lean Startup: How today's entrepreneurs use continuous innovation to create radically successful businesses*, Crown Business.

Robertson, S. and Robertson, J. (2012) *Mastering the requirements process (3e)*, Addison-Wesley Professional.

Robinson, W.L. (1974) 'Conscious competency — the mark of a competent instructor' in *Personnel Journal*, 53, pp. 538-9.

Root, R.W. and Draper, S. (1983) 'Questionnaires as a software evaluation tool' in *Proceedings of the SIGCHI Conference on Human Factors in Computing Systems*, Boston, MA.

Rosson, M.B., and Carroll, J.M. (2002) *Usability engineering: Scenario-based development of human-computer interaction*, San Francisco: Morgan Kaufmann.

Rüping, A. (2003) *Agile documentation: A pattern guide to producing lightweight documents for software projects*, Wiley.

Schneiderman, B. (1986) *Designing the user interface: Strategies for effective human-computer interaction*, Reading, MA: Addison-Wesley.

Shackel, B. (1991) 'Usability — context, framework, design, and evolution' in *Human factors for informatics usability*, Shackel, B. and Richardson, S. (eds.), Cambridge: Cambridge University Press, pp. 21-38.

Tidwell, J. (2010) *Designing interfaces (2e)*, O'Reilly.

Torres, R.J. (2002) *Practitioner's handbook for user interface design and development*, Upper Saddle River, NJ: Prentice Hall.

Tyldesley, D.A. (1988) 'Employing usability engineering in the development of office products' in *Computer Journal*, Vol. 31, No. 5, pp. 431-436.

Wertheimer, M. (1923) 'Laws of Organization in Perceptual Forms' ('Untersuchungen zur Lehre von der Gestalt II') in *Psychologische Forschung*, 4, pp. 301-50.

Wharton, C., Rieman, J., Lewis, C. and Polson, P. (1994) 'The cognitive walkthrough method: A practitioner's guide' in *Usability inspection methods*, Nielsen, J., and Mack, R.L. (eds.), New York: John Wiley & Sons.

Whiteside, J., Bennett, J. and Holtzblatt, K. (1988) 'Usability engineering: Our experience and evolution' in *Handbook of Human-Computer Interaction*, M. Helander (ed.), Amsterdam: North-Holland, pp. 791-817.

Index

A

I

icons **93, 103, 126**
ideas **181**
identification
    of things by means of naming **117**
ID numbers **93**
implementation details
    shielding users from **88**
implementation models **70, 87**
incentives **108**
    metrics-based **108**
income tax software **109**
incompetence **38**
inconsistency **21, 38**
incrementalism **185**
indexes **94**
    rotation of phrases **217**
information architects **27**
information architecture **130**
information space **130**
inheritance **68**
inheritance relationships **68**
inspections **40**
    checklist **237**
    standards **237**
installation **22**
instantiations **66**
integrated design **31**
integration projects **223**
intellectual curiosity **75**
intelligence **75**
intention **195**
intentions
    design **26, 40**
    in use cases **196**
interaction **25**
interaction concept **43, 127, 141**
interaction design **181**
interaction framework **136**
interaction sequence tables **198**
interaction styles **128**
intermediate users **74, 76, 215**
interpersonal dynamics **186**
interruptions **105**
interviews **49, 177**

free-flowing **49**
structured **49**
intrinsic satisfaction **109**
investment
    in usability activities **36**
iPhone **121**
ISO 9000 **186**
iteration **30, 183, 185**
iterative approaches **30**
iterative design **31**
iterative refinement **33, 35**

J

job shadowing **177**
justification
    of designs **181**

K

keyboards **81**
keyboard shortcuts **83, 93, 112**
keyword search **219**
KLM-GOMS model **100**
knowledge
    acquisition **78**
    existing **216**
    knowledge in the world vs. knowl-
        edge in the head **93**
Krug, Steve **98**

L

label-following strategy **232**
labels **26, 116**
laptop computers **95**
latency **104, 106**
law of closure **152**
law of common fate **153**
law of common region **155**
law of connected elements **156**
law of continuation **152**
law of good continuation **154**
Law of Good Gestalt **154**
Law of Prägnanz **147**
law of proximity **148**
law of similarity **150**

typos **212**

U

UML **202, 204**
    activity diagrams **202**
unconscious competence **79**
unconscious incompetence **79**
undo **20**
undo/redo **76, 236**
Unified Modelling Language (UML) **64**
unintended consequences
    of performance metrics **108**
unique identifiers **117**
uniqueness
    of names in a naming context **118**
unity **169**
Unix **94**
unpredictability **125**
unrecoverable crash **209**
unsaved state **141**
upvoting **108**
usability
    consultants **35**
    definition **19**
    evaluation **227**
    goals **227**

    running a session **229**

    techniques **228**

    metrics **60**
    problems **31**
    specialists **27**
usability testing **32, 37, 128, 227**
    labs **228**
    of help systems **217**
usage data collection **234**
usage logs **49**
usage statistics **49**
use cases **43, 58, 192**
    casual **195**
    cloud-level **195**
    fully-dressed **195**
    high-level **195**
    sea-level **195**

    subfunction-level **195**
    summary **195**
    underwater **195**
    user-goal level **195**
User-Centered Design (UCD) **30, 33**
    objections to **33**
user characteristics **50, 51, 174**
User Experience (UX)
    definition **21**
    negative **37**
    positive **123**
user interface design **31**
user observation **49, 177, 228**
    logs (protocols) **44**
user personas **52**
user requirements **174**
User Requirements Document **43**
user research **37**
users **48, 174**
    actual **30**
    primary **48**
    prospective **30**
    secondary **48**
user segments **50**
user's model **89**
user stories **42, 44, 58, 183, 192**
user tracking **234**

V

validation **140**
    errors **140**
    of assumptions **32, 49**
validation tables **207**
visibility **20, 126, 144, 205, 232, 236**
    design principle **112**
Visio **42**
visual appearance **25**
visual attention
    switching **97**
visual attributes **157, 164**
visual cues **104**
visual design **22, 143**
    framework **142**
visual elements
    properties of **157**
visual feedback **115**

visual hierarchy **163, 168**
visual tension **160**
vocabulary **85**
voice interfaces **81**
voluntary work **103**
voting **108**

W

waiting **98**
walkthroughs **198, 215**
Walmart **121**
wants **45**
warnings **210, 213**
waste **178**
waterfall model **29, 182, 184**
wayfinding **130**
web applications **138**
web communities **108**
websites **46**
weight (visual attribute) **160**
Wertheimer, Max **147**
whiteboards **42**
wikis **41**
wireframes **185**
wizards **76, 93**
work **22, 26, 54, 173**
    breakdown **82**
    manual **173**
    models of **82**
    system-supported **173**
workarounds **34, 74, 177**
work breakdown **182**
workers **34**
workflow **55, 71, 93, 174, 175, 176**
working memory **90, 98**
workplace environment **177**
work redesign **178**

Y

"You are here" indicator **134**

Z

Z-shaped scanning pattern **146**

About the author

Kevin Matz is the founder of Winchelsea Systems Ltd., a software product design consultancy, and is the designer and creator of the *ChapterLab* word processing and project management application for book authors. During his corporate career at firms in Canada and Germany, Kevin designed user interfaces for pension administration applications, multilingual content management systems, and software quality assurance tools. He has also designed and created web-based software development environments, audio applications, and games, and devised a novel software specification and implementation approach called *Design Intention Driven Programming*. Kevin blogs about usability and user experience design at his blog, *Architecting Usability*. He holds a BSc in Computer Science from the University of Victoria (Canada) and an MSc in Software Development from The Open University (UK).

Contact the author at: **kevin@winchelseasystems.com**

CPSIA information can be obtained at www.ICGtesting.com
Printed in the USA
LVOW11s2323300913

354780LV00005B/21/P